SpringerBriefs in Education

Key Thinkers in Education

Founding Editor

Paul Gibbs

Series Editors

Jayne Osgood, Middlesex University, London, UK

Labby Ramrathan, School of Education, University of KwaZulu-Natal, Durban, South Africa

This briefs series publishes compact (50 to 125 pages) refereed monographs under the editorial supervision of the Advisory Editor, Jayne Osgood, Middlesex University, London, UK and Labby Ramrathan, University of KwaZulu-Natal, Durban, South Africa. The series is founded by Professor Paul Gibbs, Middlesex University, London, UK. Each volume in the series provides a concise introduction to the life and work of a key thinker in education and allows readers to get acquainted with their major contributions to educational theory and/or practice in a fast and easy way. Both solicited and unsolicited manuscripts are considered for publication in the SpringerBriefs on Key Thinkers in Education series. Book proposals for this series may be submitted to the Editor: Lay Peng, Ang E-mail: laypeng.ang@springer.com

Alison Scott-Baumann

Paul Ricoeur

Empowering Education, Politics and Society

Alison Scott-Baumann
SOAS University of London
London, UK

ISSN 2211-1921   ISSN 2211-193X (electronic)
SpringerBriefs in Education
ISSN 2211-937X   ISSN 2211-9388 (electronic)
SpringerBriefs on Key Thinkers in Education
ISBN 978-981-99-3474-4   ISBN 978-981-99-3475-1 (eBook)
https://doi.org/10.1007/978-981-99-3475-1

© The Author(s) 2023. This book is an open access publication.

Open Access This book is licensed under the terms of the Creative Commons Attribution 4.0 International License (http://creativecommons.org/licenses/by/4.0/), which permits use, sharing, adaptation, distribution and reproduction in any medium or format, as long as you give appropriate credit to the original author(s) and the source, provide a link to the Creative Commons license and indicate if changes were made.

The images or other third party material in this book are included in the book's Creative Commons license, unless indicated otherwise in a credit line to the material. If material is not included in the book's Creative Commons license and your intended use is not permitted by statutory regulation or exceeds the permitted use, you will need to obtain permission directly from the copyright holder.

The use of general descriptive names, registered names, trademarks, service marks, etc. in this publication does not imply, even in the absence of a specific statement, that such names are exempt from the relevant protective laws and regulations and therefore free for general use.

The publisher, the authors, and the editors are safe to assume that the advice and information in this book are believed to be true and accurate at the date of publication. Neither the publisher nor the authors or the editors give a warranty, expressed or implied, with respect to the material contained herein or for any errors or omissions that may have been made. The publisher remains neutral with regard to jurisdictional claims in published maps and institutional affiliations.

This Springer imprint is published by the registered company Springer Nature Singapore Pte Ltd.
The registered company address is: 152 Beach Road, #21-01/04 Gateway East, Singapore 189721, Singapore

Preface

Speaking truth to power is not easy, and it becomes more complicated when you are the one with the power, and you are trying to talk yourself into being honest about something. It becomes even more complicated when that something is skin colour because, generally, we all want to believe we are not racist. As a white person, I enjoy many privileges and I am protected from forms of subtle and explicit discrimination experienced by many others. In order to solve such real-world inconsistencies and problems, I use philosophy to hold myself to account … but what happens when my most trusted philosopher lets me down by making the same mistake as me?

Indeed, it took me twenty years of studying Paul Ricoeur, a formidable, highly moral philosopher of impeccable credentials, to notice that he was unable to see what needed (and still needs) to be done to resolve racism.

Looking at contemporary UK university campuses, I note how universities are failing to respond to external accusations and assertions. Amidst this maelstrom, two groups are being targeted: firstly, black staff, students and those of colour and secondly, Muslim staff and students.

Firstly, on powerful media platforms and from some government voices, race as an issue is being side-lined to serve a common cry that institutional racism does not exist. In this phoney culture war those who resist and say racism is endemic in the university sector are accused of weakening British cultural heritage as vested in the Empire and its afterglow.

Secondly, racism towards Muslims clearly exists in the form of discrimination that is rationalised by counter-terror rhetoric: Islam is presented as a potentially violent ideology against whom everyone, including Muslims, must be protected.

In both cases endemic structural and pedagogic racism is often invisible to the perpetrators unless they choose to accept their own bias. In addition, these two groups have been racialised in a pseudo-political manner that obscures white bias from itself even more than before. On the campus of the University of Chicago, Paul Ricoeur was unable to see the necessity of meeting black student demands for equity, because he feared what he saw as identity politics.

My study does not do justice to other societal forms of unfairness and misrepresentation: rather, my objective herein has been to show the mechanisms that drive manipulative misuse of power with regard to these two groups in order to tackle wider racial, class-based and gender-related injustices.

To manifest these, I plait three strands together which are not all of the same length. The longest and most important is the search for racial justice; I entwine with this Ricoeur's philosophy and the state of the university as the second and third strands. In some chapters one or two strands will come to the fore more than the other(s). An amount of unplaiting takes place too, in the context of my recent understanding of my own bias blind spot: being nice to people is not good enough to manage structural racism.

Slowly, some sense of the need for reparations for slavery is emerging. What must also happen is a greater opening up of actual pathways of career opportunities, role models and access to influence. Visible improvements include active support of those from groups that underperform at university despite equivalent entry levels and ensuring that global majorities are represented in senior university positions, research activities and knowledge creation.

Talk to me by Alison Scott-Baumann. Softground etching on copper with plate tone. © The Author

London, UK	Alison Scott-Baumann

Acknowledgments

All errors are mine, and I wish to thank those who have advised me: Glenys Andall, Prof. Fareda Banda, Chris Beal, Dr. Alec Hamilton, Prof. John Holmwood, Imran Ahmed, Dr. Goncalo Marcelo, Helen Moss, Lottie Moore, Prof. Chris Norris, Dr. Elizabeth Scott-Baumann, Mike Scott-Baumann, Dr. Jim Scott-Baumann, Dr. Julia Stolyar and especially Prof. Ernst Wolff and Hasan Pandor for impeccable editing and critical reading. Collectively and individually my colleagues and friends at SOAS are the inspiration for my work.

Funding from: AHRC Follow-on fund 2001–2023 *New everyday practices of free speech on campus: Beyond racialised and religious stereotypes* AH/V010913/1.

Research fellowship and funding from: The Academy for Islam in Research and Society (AIWG) 2021–22.

Contents

1 **Introduction** 1
   1.1   Ricœur, Concerns and Objectives 1
   1.2   Economic Inequality and the Modern University: 1968
         and Today 5
   1.3   Understanding the Other 7
   1.4   Populism's Binaries and Ricœur 8
   1.5   Free Speech and 'Populism's Pincer Grip' 9
   1.6   Structure of This Book 10
   References 12

2 **The Idea of the University** 15
   2.1   The University as Marketplace 15
   2.2   Ricœur's Idea of the University 17
   2.3   Discrimination on Campus 19
   2.4   Discrimination Against Colour 20
   2.5   The Culture Wars and Wokeness 21
   2.6   Endless Distraction and Inaction 24
   2.7   Wael Hallaq 25
   2.8   Secularism and Islam 26
   References 28

3 **Communities of Inquiry** 33
   3.1   Communicating and Acting 33
   3.2   Challenging the Curriculum on Discrimination 34
   3.3   Communities of Inquiry 36
   3.4   Key Guidelines for Communities of Inquiry 37
   3.5   Practical Outcomes 41
   3.6   Group Work 42
   3.7   Rhetoric: Plato's Gorgias Dialogue 42
   3.8   Communities of Inquiry Sample: Challenging Callicles .. 45
   References 46

4	**Ricœur's Early Language, Activism and Algeria**	49
	4.1 Colonialism's Legacy in the Muslim World	49
	4.2 Young Ricœur and Colonial Influence	51
	4.3 Ricœur's Philosophical Toolkit	53
	4.4 Algeria and Empire	54
	4.5 Ricœur Versus Sartre: L'insoumission (Insubordination)	55
	4.6 Methodological Dialectics and Hermeneutics	57
	4.7 Linguistic Analysis and Structuralism as Method	59
	4.8 Activism Beyond Negation	60
	4.9 Communities of Inquiry Sample: Discussing Decolonisation	61
	References	62
5	**1968 and Campus Shock at Nanterre**	65
	5.1 What Happened in 1968?	65
	5.2 Ricœur's Commentaries on the University Crisis: 1968 and Beyond	67
	5.3 Hermeneutics of Suspicion	70
	5.4 The Changes Ricœur Wanted—Then and Now	71
	5.5 Negation and the Feminist Cause	73
	5.6 Ricœur Disappointed	75
	References	75
6	**Challenging 'Bad Infinity'**	79
	6.1 Negative Cultural Imaginings	79
	6.2 Whiteness	81
	6.3 Jim Crow	82
	6.4 The Denied Negative Debt at the Heart of Authoritarian Populism	83
	6.5 'Bad Infinity' and the Unhappy Consciousness	85
	6.6 Racism and Critical Race Theory (CRT)	90
	6.7 Racism: Can Ricœur Help?	91
	6.8 Communities of Inquiry Sample: Are Universities Perpetuating Institutional Racism?	92
	References	94
7	**The Politics of Pedagogy Leading to Polity Praxis**	99
	7.1 Transcending Binaries and Whiteness—An Outline	99
	7.2 The Fate of Activism?	100
	7.3 Factors Militating Against Communities of Inquiry	101
	7.4 Ricœurian Justice and Current UK Politics	102
	7.5 Pragmatist Probabilities	103
	7.6 Rhetorical Pragmatism	104
	7.7 Religion on Campus: The Politics of Pedagogy	106
	7.8 Polity Praxis: German Case Study on Religious Thinking	107
	7.9 The Politics of Pedagogy: Influencing the Corridors of Power	108

	7.10 Polity Praxis: An All-Party Parliamentary Group	109
	References	110
8	**Conclusion**	113
	References	117
Index		119

Chapter 1
Introduction

Abstract This introductory chapter provides a personal testimony about how I, the author, late in life, experience better understanding of white privilege and its distortion of reality within daily life and philosophy than philosopher Paul Ricœur apparently did. Nevertheless, Ricœur's dialectical approach can be used to analyse and understand personal and group needs and identity. Thus philosophy can provide clarity if it also accepts critique. I bring a pragmatist philosophy of free speech: this is a threefold model of nested Russian dolls (as an analogy) to show how three progressively more outward facing forms of discussion can provide a model for better communication. I call them, respectively: *Communities of Inquiry*, the politics of pedagogy and polity praxis. In addition, *Communities of Inquiry* (the smallest doll yet the core to it all) is comprised of a fourfold typology of speech which moves from libertarian to liberal to guarded liberal and finally to no platforming. This chapter also sketches the economic and social changes that provide a backdrop for the current turmoil in the higher education sector.

Keywords Bias blind spot · Colonialism · Culture war · Free speech · Identity politics · Matryoshka dolls · Populism's pincer grip · Whiteness

1.1 Ricœur, Concerns and Objectives

As part of a series on great thinkers and their approaches to education, this book is about the important French philosopher Paul Ricœur[1] (1913–2005) and the relevance of his work for improving the state of higher education in Britain in the 2020s. I will compare and contrast Ricœur's struggles in two different university systems—mid twentieth century France and late twentieth century USA, especially the University of Chicago—with current issues around populism on UK campuses.

Historically, binary populist arguments have often proposed that government is corrupt and that the people's needs are suffering (Mudde and Kaltwasser 2017). Currently, a different populist argument is deployed by politicians, the media and

---

[1] Pronounce 'recur' and roll your 'r's.

© The Author(s) 2023
A. Scott-Baumann, *Paul Ricoeur*,
SpringerBriefs on Key Thinkers in Education,
https://doi.org/10.1007/978-981-99-3475-1_1

their allies: seeking to deflect attention from increasing demands to tackle historical wrongs such as slavery, they argue, through the waging of a 'culture war', that there is a corrupting force *on campus* that vilifies the white public's cultural heritage (such as the history of empire). A culture war is a conflict between groups (often liberal versus conservative) over the nature and values of the cultural heritage to which they both lay claim. Another term that can be used is free speech wars, whereby a populist binary is created between unrestricted free speech (libertarianism) and the silencing of free speech (no platforming). To analyse these binaries, I will draw on Ricœur's strengths (using language constructively, helping us to challenge populism and its binaries, aspiring to a rich learning and teaching environment for all) whilst also highlighting his limitations (appearing unable or unwilling to apply his ideas on mutual recognition to American students' attempts to reduce racism and discrimination). As an older white woman, I have researched Ricœur for twenty years, and have been impressed and comforted by his balanced, irenic approach to selfhood, society and linguistic awareness. Ricœur developed a form of philosophical anthropology that attempts to balance identity and alterity and pours energy into understanding the dissymmetry that characterizes human relationships. His philosophy is characterized by humility, spirituality and an insatiable longing for unattainable wholeness.

Ricoeur is important to the question of the way potentially incendiary subjects are discussed on campus, because he was at the heart of the 1968 events in French universities, in which the response to entrenched positions, and a sense of injustice and imbalance between students and the teaching staff (and, beyond them, the government), led to riots, destruction and a painful and gradual reaching towards a truce-like resolution. Exactly these same potent conflicts are present in today's British universities, and yet they are failing to spur protest.

So, in our current predicament, is his approach enough? One of the most fundamental socio-political issues today is the nexus of free speech, identity politics and university funding problems, which are set against the backdrop of the nasty perseverance of marginalization, systemic violence and brutal racialized othering. Faced with this, I now finally understand that there is a discrepancy between Ricœur's capacity to unify ideas and his failure to understand human difference. Having disingenuously thought for decades that my supposedly non-racist kindness will suffice to remedy systemic discrimination, I now see that I have secretly known about my privilege all my life, which triggers the urgent need to acknowledge and act upon my bias in a much more explicit way. Perhaps I should have read George Lipsitz's *The Possessive Investment in Whiteness* (Lipsitz 1998), which demonstrates how public policy and private need combine to protect the needs of the dominant, mostly white, groups; but maybe I would still not have seen the need to act. I can appreciate how I allowed myself to make the same mistakes Ricœur did, because of not experiencing negative, racially-rooted discrimination. In Britain and in Europe I have never feared being, nor will I ever be, subjected to 'stop and search' by police. I will never be racially profiled while seeking access to the House of Commons in Westminster. I will never be physically attacked because of the colour of my skin. When I arrive at the university campus, I am never mistaken for a cleaner when I am in fact a university professor. In Europe, I am white and privileged; globally, I am part of a minority who behave like a majority. I propose we can learn from Ricœur's and my bias blind spot, which protected us both from understanding the personal role white people play in discrimination and racism.

Ricœur offers us a philosophy for higher education that is based upon his enduring belief that we can, and indeed must, honour the urgent need for us all to communicate better with each other and with ourselves. He was an anti-colonial activist in the Franco-Algerian colonial debate and later worked with government as an advisor on issues such as citizenship and migration. Ricœur protested openly with students and academics at the Sorbonne about the torture in Algeria and the urgent need for the French to liberate Algeria. We will see in the chapter on Nanterre (Chap. 5) that he fully supported the student leaders in their demands for negotiation, despite misgivings about the efficacy of such a process. Yet in the chapter on the USA (Chap. 6), I show that he felt discomfort about identity politics being used as a basis for protest. Thus, I will show that some forty years after his fight against French colonialism in Algeria, he was unable to deal with the repercussions of American subjugation of peoples of colour through slavery. When global majority students[2] made demands for recognition on US campuses, his understanding and responses were inadequate. This response shows a lack of awareness about the powerful praxis developed in Chicago during his time there by black students, students of Latin-American heritage and middle-class white students to mobilise groups not only on campus but across all communities in order to correct injustices. This is a model that could be followed to considerable benefit in the UK. Solidarity can only develop when white populations acknowledge the privilege they secretly know they have, and accept that the economy, the environment and society are in desperate and urgent need of solidarity across groups that will facilitate activism currently inhibited by so-called 'culture wars'.

Despite Ricœur's failure to act, his dialectical approach (identifying and moderating the antagonistic effects of the false binaries we use to shape our understanding) stands strong and is urgently needed in the 2020s to challenge the way in which British universities are being squeezed by a pincer grip formed of libertarians in government and no-platformers on campus; Ricœur's work provides antidotes and counter arguments to both these extremisms in this culture war in which the libertarian nationalist wants to 'protect' British traditions from the multicultural 'modernizing' impulses of the no-platformer. Depending on your view, one position is positive and the other is negative. Ricœur advocated avoiding quick decision-making, preferring extensive discussion of one argument against another, and he proposed that all decisions must be provisional because circumstances and contexts change. His dialectical position challenged both Hegel, who attempted to make too little of the negative by cancelling it out (Hegel 1991), and Horkheimer and Adorno who arguably made too much of the negatives faced by modern Europe post World War 2 (Horkheimer and Adorno 2002). Instead, for Ricœur, as I will show, it is the interplay of both negative and positive that is important.

---

[2] I use the term global majority because, although people of colour are considered a minority in the US and UK, they form a majority across our planet.

What makes Ricœur's work invaluable despite its flaws, is that it is premised on an affirmative humanism that can help us to rediscover the power of debate; and yet, the caveat must be added, it is not enough in this time of what Edward Said called the 'reductive and vulgarizing us-versus-them' model (Said 2004, 50). In his 2023 book *Not So Black and White*, Kenan Malik describes a different yet related binary: the tension between 'a desire to push out and create a more universal perspective and a retreat into a narrow, racialized sense of identity' (Malik 2023, 226); he also provides an analysis of 'the reactionary roots of much contemporary radical identity politics' (Malik 2023, 276). I propose to show in my book that such tensions are in fact core to our being but that Ricœur represents them in ways that preclude resolution. We must accept dichotomies, but also push back against those who exaggerate these polarizations in inflammatory ways. I will show, for example, how the prevalent rhetoric of a culture war confected by state actors and media confuses us and silences our attempts to achieve some sort of balance between our personal and group needs and identities. To achieve such balance we need to understand universalism as giving more support than we might think reasonable to those who suffer the racialisation of society.

To deal with these us-versus-them pincer grips, I propose supplementing Ricœur's dialectical method with three interrelated levels of action, each of which requires that we believe in our personal agency to use the power of language for discussing, explaining and understanding better in order to act well. My strategy to resolve this is to apply a threefold model: three interdependent ways of exercising personal agency, using Ricoeur's faith in the power of language. Think of a Russian doll (they are called Matryoshka dolls), where one large wooden doll conceals within her a smaller doll, and that doll within her a yet smaller one, and so on. In this analogy, *Communities of Inquiry* (CofI) (see Sect. 3.3) is the smallest doll at the heart of a set of three. She shows the necessity of open yet commonly agreed discussion in any situation in which we find ourselves. The larger doll she sits in is the 'politics of pedagogy', which is the *Influencing the Corridors of Power* (ICOP) project (see Sect. 7.9). When we unite in a politics of pedagogy, we take the learning and teaching outside the classroom into parliament and the wider world, a place where politics is about being a person who challenges the epistemic injustice of not being considered to have valid views and learns how to interact with politicians and groups outside the university. This is also one of the moral technologies for what I call polity praxis, the largest of the three dolls and the most encompassing pragmatist approach to a better society: this is the *All-Party Parliamentary Group (APPG) Communities of Inquiry across the Generations* (see Sect. 7.10). Through polity praxis citizens without party-political positions can become part of the political debate and bring both their demands and their expertise into policymaking. At these second and third levels, I propose activist engagement with parliament and with policymakers that reduces the democratic deficit by improving political literacy amongst university students and staff. In the current politicised climate of education, this activism takes place at the intersection of education, politics, culture and nationalism. Young Ricœur engaged in such activism; older Ricœur did not.

Focusing on the first of these three dolls, *Communities of Inquiry* has a fourfold typology of positions for pragmatist discussions: liberal, guarded liberal, libertarian and no-platforming. The liberal and guarded liberal approaches to discussion (with occasional use of libertarian approaches) have been the discourse styles that universities have traditionally prided themselves on: liberalism (i.e. free discussion within legal limits on the assumption—possibly unfounded—of general agreement in a group) can be replaced by guarded liberalism to take account of possible cultural, gendered, religious or ethnic differences of opinion. No-platforming is the extreme version of the guarded liberal approach, which can now be found in class and around campus, reflecting the increasing tendency to avoid using language that could cause upset or offence rather than exploring differences to resolve them; the assumption is that the discussion itself may harm minority groups, and they ought to be afforded particular protection. For example, in class and around campus it has recently become difficult to discuss gender identity, and especially transgender identity—a difficulty which perpetuates confusion and negativity. Libertarians, on the other hand, assert in an equally damaging way that we all have the right to speak as freely as we wish, even if we upset others, or precisely because we can. Recourse to this fourfold typology (liberal, guarded liberal, libertarian and no-platforming) ensures that the parameters for dealing with offence are clear, and it is a helpful mechanism to explore the topics raised in this book, which include free speech, racism, Islamophobia and the state of the university sector.

1.2 Economic Inequality and the Modern University: 1968 and Today

To explore these topics, the 2020s English university system will provide the context; yet it is worth noting that 1968 was a tumultuous year in many universities across the world as they provided a heady atmosphere for children born after World War 2 who wanted to right the social and cultural wrongs that faced them in the societies they were born into (Reader and Wadia 1993).

In 1968 Robert Kennedy and Martin Luther King were assassinated, Vietnam war protests reached a peak and the Tet offensive in Vietnam demonstrated America's weakness. There is an important economic background too. In 1966, financial markets worldwide had suffered the first (largely unknown and unnoticed) post-war crash: it emanated from America and set the pattern for future instability in money markets worldwide with a toxic combination of fast financial technology, slow regulation and cunning banks (Stepek 2017). This created a lending boom followed by a shortage of money.

Students took recourse to protest and affiliation with progressive politics to demand correctives for racism, human rights violations, foreign wars, economic difficulties and the hegemony of empire, with protests bubbling up on campuses in North and South America, Europe and Japan. Some of these 1968 protests were effective in ways that seem unimaginable in 2023: together, French students and trade unions nearly brought the country to a standstill as President de Gaulle briefly fled France. By contrast, today, increased levels of surveillance, censorship and restrictions on protest severely limit the opportunities and prospects for students to demand change, especially in China, India and Russia where protest is brutally suppressed, but also in the countries I focus on herein: France, the UK and the US.

France resolved its 1968 crisis; yet the economic difficulties were just beginning and they have since become much worse. In his *Brief History of Equality*, French economist Thomas Piketty shows us that we, in capitalist nation states, are held hostage by our own inability (and our governments' unwillingness) to redistribute wealth in ways that are equitable, fair and universally productive (Piketty 2022). Although for thirty years after the Second World War, an equitable redistribution of wealth in capitalist nation states seemed attainable, by the 1970s the combination of wars and unequal taxation systems favoured the very rich; this led to ever-growing increases in inequalities that have not been reversed since. In addition, it is now clear that much of the huge, accumulated wealth and privilege of that minority of economically powerful people—the middle classes and the very rich 1%—can be traced back to the wealth accumulated from empires we thought were dead (Savage 2021). Moreover, as Savage explains in *The Return of Inequality: Social Change and the Weight of the Past*, this wealth is perpetuated by patterns of exploitation that resemble imperial ideologies, as seen for example in the way cities dominate their surroundings and are under heavy surveillance, and which host gated communities to protect the rich, but which are serviced by the poor, including students, many of whom are in long term debt (Savage 2021).

The modern British university is much changed from 50 years ago and is in crisis: it is constrained in the money it can spend, the language it can use and the subjects it can teach, and it has been marketized to provide a serviced product. The mood in wider society is volatile, as is manifested in populist accusation and counter-accusation, social media addiction, insult and propagandist shouting, as well as a cost-of-living crisis that shows how weakened civil society has become. We define ourselves currently more by the degree of offence we cause each other than by the degree of affection we feel for each other. The modern university now serves a larger, more representative student population than it previously has done; yet, remarkably, the university sector is unwilling, unable or unready to respond to the heated debates around democracy, free speech and race. Structural racism is real: in 2020, 38.2% of white graduates were awarded a first-class degree, compared with 19.1% of black graduates. This does, however, mark a discernible improvement since in the last six years the percentage gap between white and black graduates being awarded a first class or a 2.1 degree went down from 26.3 to 20.0% (UCAS 2022; Higher Education Statistics Agency 2022). Progress, nevertheless, is slow and the government denies structural racism despite clear evidence to the contrary (Campbell 2022). The university sector is also losing its funding for arts and humanities subjects, where counternarratives to such denials could traditionally find expression. All the while, Wilhelm von Humboldt's nineteenth century dream of an Enlightenment campus where cool true wisdom is nurtured through teaching underpinned by research is still secretly aspired to by many academics.

1.3 Understanding the Other

Ricœur developed powerful arguments about our constant need, as he saw it, to understand ourselves by how we understand the other and how we see ourselves reflected in the other. In this book I apply his ideas to two groups that are frequently 'othered' on British university campuses: Muslim students and staff and black students and staff (I will also use the term people of colour). Black and white are racialized terms bound up with the history of torment or privilege endowed by societies upon skin colour. Muslim groups are thought to be dangerous and are subjected to the state's relentless application of an anti-extremist lens which has a chilling effect on freedom of expression. Students and staff of colour are thought to be somehow inferior and are increasingly exposed to the effects of libertarian populist attacks upon those features of HE that attempt to reduce systemic racism (decolonisation, diversity training and antiracism initiatives). With both groups we witness how the freedom of expression of some will curtail the freedom of expression, if not the silencing, of others.

To address these issues, we need to challenge Ricoeur's approach. As a universalist, he avoided dealing with the realities of individuals' experiences of racism. Instead, he preferred to set these in a broader, more abstract context—the 'human condition', and the tendencies discernible in people's actions, irrespective of their colour. However, owing to distortions of history, we experience others and are experienced differently by them depending on skin colour, facial features, religion and gender—and the politics of the culture wars and populism exacerbate this. We thus need to consider how the less heard voice can express itself—in the ways it would authentically choose—in linguistic and social contexts controlled by another with a history of domination. This may include women students wanting to speak in seminars, Muslims on campus seeking not to be labelled as terrorists, black students hoping not to be academically underestimated by their skin colour, and Jewish students who do not wish to be measured solely by their views on Zionism. Ricœur's universalist conciliatory ideas about our moral use of language are not enough: they require the practical scaffolding of the pragmatist tradition, which insists upon taking the individual human perspective seriously and exploring the ways in which our personal beliefs and habits influence our behaviour and vice versa. I juxtapose his work at the University of Chicago with that of early pragmatist, Jane Addams (1860–1935), whose community-based practices in her work with migrants in Chicago created a template for the 'community of inquiry' (Addams 1910). Addams was a forerunner to feminist standpoint epistemology in implementing her belief that knowledge is in many ways contextual and gendered and that the wider context is the community. I will also use the work of university professor Danielle Allen who recommends political friendship, personal sacrifice and the bold use of rhetoric in anti-discriminatory endeavours in her book *Talking to strangers* (Allen 2004), which she wrote when based at the University of Chicago.

By complementing Ricœur's work with the pragmatist approaches of Addams and Allen, the *Communities of Inquiry* model I propose is more of an organising principle than a method and is based upon two beliefs that deserve reinvigoration after having been weakened and sidelined by the dominance of political ideologies based upon accusatory antagonisms. The first tenet of a *Community of Inquiry* is that it is both necessary and worthwhile to discuss intractable problems with a view to finding some sort of resolution; and second, that procedural ethics (clear, morally grounded, mutually agreed guidelines for conversational conduct) are paramount both for enabling productive discussion and also for understanding these intractable problems.

1.4 Populism's Binaries and Ricœur

In order to conceal state-imposed hardships, authoritarian populism's brutal binaries demand adversarial non-cooperation and create a militant 'law and order' rhetoric in opposition to a rights agenda. Stuart Hall explains how 'to raise the question of rights and civil liberties is tantamount to declaring oneself a "subversive"' (Hall 2021: 79–80). Creating and adopting false binaries and aggressively negating the opposing position creates adversarial stalemates. Such wrangling destroys the two classical pillars of rational or even sensible thought: first, if we want to understand ourselves and others, we need propositions that are non-contradictory; and second, these propositions should cohere as part of a recognisable argument with which every party can engage.

At the same time, contradictory binaries are a key feature of human thought. We often seek to understand something by contrasting it with something else, creating dualism that can guide a form of discussion, a dialectic. The binary can become a form of dualism, such that each pole is defined by its difference from the other; for example, secularism is often defined by its relation to religion. This can create distortion as each often becomes an exaggerated version of itself to ensure that it seems different enough.

Binaries are also instrumental to Ricœur's technique for creating understanding, but he was always sensitive to the need to choose binaries that have something in common, without which no resolution would be possible. By deploying dialectic in Ricœur's way, which is to develop two views in tension with each other, we can better understand how populism works. We can seek to understand and critique authoritarian populism, and then attenuate it, turning it into a positive, less authoritarian version than that identified by Stuart Hall (Hall 2021).

Another advantage of Ricoeur's dialectical approach is that it seeks to also understand the other (i.e. the interlocutor), as can be explored through his dialectic of event and meaning. Ricœur posits that the event of a verbal utterance is inadequate to the task of communicating fully to another person the meaning of being *you*; yet, somehow, some understanding of individual identity can be transmitted linguistically so that the other can derive *some* understanding of the incommunicable meaning of what it means to be another person (Ricœur 1976, 14–17).

Ricœur's dialectical approach constitutes another thread throughout this book, and in Sect. 4.6 I specifically consider how it helps us challenge populist binaries and see the relevance of dialectical debate for productive conversations.

1.5 Free Speech and 'Populism's Pincer Grip'

In England, populist influence has created a wider tendency for freedom of speech to be understood in binary terms, as the right to express a personal opinion with no consequences whatsoever (libertarianism), or, conversely and perversely, no right to express an opinion at all (no-platforming). University campuses have become a key site for this free speech crisis, with Conservative politicians complaining about the cultural influence of universities, asserting that they are full of left wing no-platforming extremists who deny a platform to those with different views from their own (Fazackerley 2020); having asserted their concerns, these politicians then curb universities' freedoms and influence through legislation. This, and societal discrimination result in corresponding reactions from those committed to the protection of minorities and/ or to the voicing of histories unheard, and this can lead to expressions of extreme sensitivity being articulated poorly. The HE sector seems to be mesmerized and trapped by this pincer grip in which the right wing feels it imperative to deny that racism and discrimination exist, while the left wing insists that racism and discrimination exist everywhere; I call this phenomenon 'Populism's Pincer Grip'.

At the time of writing, the UK Conservative government's campaign to create a narrative in competition with the universities' perceived leftism can be found in the 2023 Higher Education (Freedom of Speech) Act[3] that insists completely free speech for all, thereby removing the commitment to eliminate discrimination provided by the Equality Act (Renton and Scott-Baumann 2021). At the crux of this libertarian absolutism are the following four assertions: institutional racism does not exist; diversity training is not only unnecessary but actually counterproductive; the rights of minorities will, accordingly, not need to be protected; free speech is at risk if any or all of the aforementioned are challenged. Indeed, planned changes to the data protection law and rights legislation 2022 will go far beyond the university sector and affect the UK, by 'placing freedom of speech above the right to privacy in a way which unbalances the relationship between competing rights, potentially undermining people's ability to enforce their privacy rights (see Clause 4 of the Bill of Rights Bill)' [4] (Duhs 2022). Yet, in Ricœur's words,

---

[3] https://www.legislation.gov.uk/ukpga/2023/16/enacted

[4] https://publications.parliament.uk/pa/bills/cbill/58-03/0117/220117.pdf. At the time of writing (early 2023) the Bill is at the 2nd reading stage in the House of Commons: https://bills.parliament.uk/bills/3227.

the independent exercise of justice and the independent formation of opinion are the two lungs of a politically sound state. Without these, there is asphyxiation. (Ricœur 1965, 268)

In that spirit, I will show how universities can hold the government to account by working actively to explore, monitor and comment upon planned legislation.

As well as using Ricœur's philosophy, I will draw upon statistical evidence of social trends in Britain and the USA regarding the key issues that I address. We all have access to large samples that reflect our cultural imagination and often show how wrong we are in our ideas about each other. Typically unresponsive to more accurate counter evidence, these misshapen ideas are often systemic, society-wide beliefs as we see, for example, with common societal convictions about immigration being a major problem (Duffy 2019, 106–16). Both such statistically analysed 'facts' and philosophical ideas are subjective in their own ways; I hope they will complement each other in some sort of dialectical balance, which is one of my methodological recommendations.

1.6 Structure of This Book

Here, in this chapter, I begin several threads that flow throughout the book, engaging directly with some of those who are 'othered' and with writers who represent them. Consideration of Islam on campus, of racism on campus and (to an extent) of identity issues on campus, will show tragically unresolved tensions. In order to attempt resolution of such matters, it will be necessary to go beyond Ricœur, and I turn to the pragmatism of Jane Addams (intensely practical, face-to-face engagement and action research) and of Frank Ramsey (intensely cerebral yet practical engagement with human reasoning), as well as the approach of Danielle Allen, which is based upon personal sacrifice and use of Aristotelian rhetoric. I propose my own version of academic activism.

In Chap. 2, I consider some of the key issues that beset universities in the twenty-first century and contrast them with Ricœur's interventions in the 1960s; as a comparator, 1968 seems as if it was a very innocent time for higher education.

In Chap. 3, I provide a definition of 'free speech' as a negotiated process, and consider how, using the *Communities of Inquiry* (CofI) approach, young people can relearn the art of discussion as they progress through university. A politics of pedagogy entails each teacher and each student becoming a facilitator: the individuals develop a group narrative and learn from each other in ways that create group identity based on sharing the risk of offending each different other. The politics of pedagogy is also the ability to have debate both inside and outside the university and talk, as a group as well as individually, to activists and thinktanks, to politicians, policymakers and civil servants and to convene *Communities of Inquiry*.

The next three chapters (4, 5 and 6) explore Ricœur's intellectual development with specific focus upon his views on higher education. These chapters use historical evidence to extrapolate conceptual changes in him and in society. They will show

1.6 Structure of This Book   11

increasingly how he was not able to address, or was not interested in, the pragmatism that necessitates the presence of the body as integral to the solutions sought, not least because of bodily characteristics such as skin colour.

Chapter 4 explores how, from 1947, with increasing anger, he worked with students to oppose colonial France in Algeria, culminating in his house arrest in 1961. As a junior academic, Ricœur held utopian ideas about the university as a site for self-development and rich educational opportunities for all, as well as a locus for political activism. As a relatively junior academic, his approach, based on polemical discussion and activism with students as well as postwar idealism, was successful over the issue of Algeria.

Chapter 5 explores his later attempts during the 1968–71 student rebellions to engage with students through discussion. In the mid-1960s he sought an alternative higher education model to break the higher education hegemony of the Sorbonne as a place of huge lectures and distant tutors. He was sympathetic to the students' rebelliousness; yet their impassioned rhetoric took them onto the streets and Ricœur's bookish approach was rendered mute. Ricœur's dream of equality of class, gender and subject discipline on campus was not realized, and his interventions metamorphosed into abject failures.

In Chapter 6, I consider how, despite his admiration for the collegial American campus, Ricœur became wary of attempts by minority groups on campus to supplant discrimination with respect and recognition for their difference. Drawing upon his experiences in the USA, we see that he understood the twentieth-century campus to be a site of racism, and that the university sector (like himself) had failed to challenge and resolve it. Contrasts are drawn with the University of Chicago student movements which offer a powerful model of united activism on campus and beyond. They often failed but the idea of solidarity across class, colour and creed must be the only way forward. Influenced perhaps to an extent by French assimilationism, he believed that demands from those discriminated against and their escalation in intensity were correspondingly less likely to lead to mutual recognition.

In Chapter 7, my incorporation of Ricœur's and Addams' conciliatory work into *Communities of Inquiry* offers a clear way to transform the modern university into a locus of active political engagement with the outside world, as I will evidence through my work on democratic literacy, namely the *Influencing the Corridors of Power* (ICOP) project based at SOAS, University of London, and the *All-Party Parliamentary Group* (APPG) called *Communities of Inquiry across the Generations* based in Westminster[5]; whilst ICOP enlarges the scope of the CofI approach with the politics of pedagogy, the APPG aspires to polity praxis, the widest scope of citizens speaking evidence-based truths in the corridors of power.

Each chapter shows historical and conceptual connections between Ricœur's work and university-related social events on and off campus. We can learn a great deal both from his powerful analysis of how to understand the other and, conversely, over the decades, his progressively more remarkable inability to see the necessity of resolving racialized tensions. In order to implement Ricœur's focus upon the other, I

---

[5] https://blogs.soas.ac.uk/cop/.

draw upon my research with Muslim groups and the research and literature on racism: of course, class, gender and other areas also desperately need resolving, but Muslims and people of colour have been nominated by current right-wing movements as the 'other', to be vilified and tormented, while at the same time denying any such thing, and these are thus my focus in this short book. To help us replace the simplistic binaries of right-wing populist rhetoric and protective left-wing rights moves that shut down conversation, we need to talk.

References

Addams, Jane. 1910. *Twenty Years at Hull-House*. New York: Macmillan.
Allen, Danielle S. 2004. *Talking to Strangers: Anxieties of Citizenship since Brown v. Board of Education*. Chicago, Illinois: University of Chicago Press.
Campbell, Paul I. 2022. 'Pray(ing) the person marking your work isn't racist': Racialised inequities in HE assessment practice. *Teaching in Higher Education*. https://doi.org/10.1080/13562517.2022.2119075.
Duffy, Bobby. 2019. *Why We're Wrong about Nearly Everything: A Theory of Human Misunderstanding*. First. US. New York, NY: Basic Books.
Duhs, Eleonor. 2022. 'Changes to Data Protection Law and the Risks to the UK Economy'. Academic. *SOAS Influencing the Corridors of Power* (blog). 5 September 2022. https://blogs.soas.ac.uk/cop/wp-content/uploads/2022/09/SOAS-ICOP-Brief-Data-Protection-and-Digital-Information.pdf.
Fazackerley, Anna. 2020. "McCarthyism in the UK': Academics Fear Shaming for Leftwing Views'. *The Guardian*, 10 March 2020, sec. Education. https://www.theguardian.com/education/2020/mar/10/mccarthyism-uk-universities-academics-fear-shaming-for-leftwing-views.
Hall, Stuart. 2021. *Selected Writings on Race and Difference*. Edited by Paul Gilroy and Ruth Wilson Gilmore. Stuart Hall: Selected Writings. Durham: Duke University Press.
Hegel, G. W. F. 1991.*The Encyclopaedia Logic: Part I of the Encyclopaedia of the Philosophical Sciences with the Zustze*. UK edition. Indianapolis: Hackett Publishing Company.
Higher Education Statistics Agency. 2022. 'Undergraduate Degree Results'. Official Statistics. UK: Higher Education Statistics Agency. https://www.ethnicity-facts-figures.service.gov.uk/education-skills-and-training/higher-education/undergraduate-degree-results/latest.
Horkheimer, Max, and Theodor W. Adorno. 2002. *Dialectic of Enlightenment*. Translated by Edmund Jephcott. Stanford: Stanford University Press.
Lipsitz, George. 1998. *The Possessive Investment in Whiteness: How White People Profit from Identity Politics*. Philadelphia: Temple University Press, U.S.
Malik, Kenan. 2023. *Not So Black and White: A History of Race from White Supremacy to Identity Politics*. London: C Hurst & Co Publishers Ltd.
Mudde, Cas, and Cristóbal Rovira. Kaltwasser. 2017. *Populism: A Very Short Introduction*, 2nd ed. New York, NY: OUP USA.
Piketty, Thomas. 2022. *A brief history of equality*. Translated by Steven Rendall.
Reader, Keith A., and Khursheed Wadia. 1993. 'Women and the Events of May 1968'. In *The May 1968 Events in France: Reproductions and Interpretations*. Eds. Keith A. Reader and Khursheed Wadia, 148–66. London: Palgrave Macmillan UK. https://doi.org/10.1007/978-1-349-22702-0_6.
Renton, David, and Alison Scott-Baumann. 2021. 'The HE Free Speech Bill Must Incorporate the Equality Act'. Academic. *SOAS Influencing the Corridors of Power* (blog). 19 July 2021. https://blogs.soas.ac.uk/cop/wp-content/uploads/2021/07/The-HE-free-speech-bill-must-incorporate-the-Equality-Act-July-2021-3.pdf.

References

Ricœur, Paul. 1965. *History and Truth: Translated with an Introduction by Charles A. Kelbley.* Translated by Charles A. Kelbey. 2nd ed. Evanston, IL: Northwestern University Press.

Ricœur, Paul. 1976. *Interpretation theory: discourse and the surplus of meaning.* Fort Worth: Texas Christian University Press.

Said, Edward W. 2004. *Humanism and Democratic Criticism.* Columbia Themes in Philosophy. New York: Columbia University Press.

Savage, Michael. 2021. *The Return of Inequality: Social Change and the Weight of the Past.* Cambridge, Massachusetts; London: Harvard University Press.

Scott-Baumann, Alison, and Simon Perfect. 2021. *Freedom of Speech in Universities Islam, Charities and Counter-Terrorism.* Islam in the World. London & New York: Routledge, Taylor & Francis Group.

Stepek, John. 2017. 'How the Credit Crunch of 1966 Set the Tone for Central Banks'. *MoneyWeek*, 18 August 2017. https://moneyweek.com/471592/how-the-credit-crunch-of-1966-set-the-tone-for-central-banks.

UCAS. 2022. 'Entry Rates into Higher Education'. UCAS End of Cycle Report. UK: Universities and Colleges Admissions Service. https://www.ethnicity-facts-figures.service.gov.uk/education-skills-and-training/higher-education/entry-rates-into-higher-education/latest#main-facts-and-figures

Open Access This chapter is licensed under the terms of the Creative Commons Attribution 4.0 International License (http://creativecommons.org/licenses/by/4.0/), which permits use, sharing, adaptation, distribution and reproduction in any medium or format, as long as you give appropriate credit to the original author(s) and the source, provide a link to the Creative Commons license and indicate if changes were made.

The images or other third party material in this chapter are included in the chapter's Creative Commons license, unless indicated otherwise in a credit line to the material. If material is not included in the chapter's Creative Commons license and your intended use is not permitted by statutory regulation or exceeds the permitted use, you will need to obtain permission directly from the copyright holder.

Chapter 2
The Idea of the University

Abstract This chapter explores some of the key issues that have beset English universities in the twenty first century with a summary of some key areas in Ricœur's early philosophy and interventions in the 1960s. Comparisons and contrasts are made from the 1960s with current debates about free speech on campus in England: complaints from 2017 to 2022 from outside the university about both more and less free speech have multiplied, whilst there has been increasingly less discussion *inside* the university about how to converse well. Equality, diversity and inclusion are policy labels that are in conflict with Prevent, the UK's counterterror programme targeted at 'extremist' ideas that are nonetheless lawful.

Keywords EDI · Habermas · Hallaq · Prevent · 'Woke'

2.1 The University as Marketplace

In his 1968 preface to *Conceptions de l'université* (*Designing the University*), Paul Ricœur quoted with approval Karl Jaspers' assertion that the university must be a place where teachers and their students can search for the truth together without constraint (Ricœur 1968a, 10); but Ricœur wondered if this idea was becoming problematic. He further mused that even if we decided this idea was not being upheld in good faith by European governments, it would still be necessary to retain the university, in order for us to be able to interrogate the *possibility* of free thought. He was optimistic that everyone should have access to university to discuss ideas openly. Fifty years on we are compelled to ask whether the university is still recognisable as a place for ideas and varieties of truth: 'the pursuit of truth,' Abdal Hakim Murad reflects, 'now seems set at the margins, thanks to the monetizing of the academy, or because of hyper specialisation and weak interdisciplinarity, or because of the ambient post-modernising culture in which the pursuit of truth is simply dismissed as a fool's errand' (Murad 2020, 237).

There are many instructive contrasts between Ricœur's dually idealistic and pragmatic understanding of the liberal university campus in 1968, and its realities in the 2020s. Four major factors delineate these differences. First, mass education has become a reality in many parts of the world. Second, funding this vastly expanded sector has become problematic, and also less prioritised by governments. This results in students becoming indebted consumers of educational services and compromises the quality of education delivered, such as the quasi-colleges described in *Universities and Colleges: A Very Short Introduction* by Palfreyman and Temple (2017, 85). When higher education becomes a private investment in human capital, the market approach becomes the main issue. Third, the campus is inevitably affected by dramatic societal transformations which include the cultural dominance of digital communication, distance learning methods, and the growth of identity politics from outside the university, particularly via political activism, as an attempt to right the historical wrongs that democracies fail to address. The fourth major difference is the 'chilling' of speech, the well-documented self-censorship by staff and students worried about being thought extremist if they discuss Islam or racism or Israel/Palestine or gender identity with different views from those promoted by the government (Townend 2017; Scott-Baumann et al. 2020).

In the 1960s, Ricœur predicted marketization of mass education, but could not have foreseen the scale of it. Market dominance and free market models have become key factors in commercialising education: in 2012 English and Welsh university fees trebled, with the 'justification' that the quality of higher education is commensurate with graduate earnings. By suggesting a sliding scale of student fees, the government sought to create competition amongst universities, but, unsurprisingly, most universities charged maximum fees. Thus, in 2013, the cap on student recruitment was removed: this led to huge over-recruitment by ambitious universities—even when they did not have the capacity to cope; and universities that did not seek to expand rapidly were financially weakened. In 2016, a 'teaching excellence framework' was introduced, which spurred endeavours to differentiate between courses that are deemed good/poor value for money.

As it is, under the current English system, 'universities don't bear the cost of failure [...and] graduates are insured against bad outcomes'; nevertheless, on average graduates do earn 'significantly' more over a lifetime, and 'sending about half of young people to university is a good deal overall for the taxpayer' (Johnson 2020). Arts and humanities degrees were designated 'low value', and their funding was drastically reduced,[1] whereas funding for Science, Technology, Engineering and Maths (STEM subjects) remains healthy (Bulaitis 2021). There has also been a significant drop in students studying languages, both foreign and English: the drop in the former was inevitable due to the huge reduction in teaching provisions for it in schools over the last 20 years, but English too has witnessed a drop by a third over the decade from 2011 (Davies 2022, 8). Various mechanisms of complex audits and assessments such as the Research Excellence Framework (REF) are forcing universities to compete with each other—which takes energy and resources from the teaching and research aspects of university life. This leaves little energy to critique

---

[1] From £36 million to £19 million for arts courses in the academic year 2021–2022 (Bulaitis 2021).

the neoliberal system that has co-opted universities into submission (Jones 2022, 248).

However, back in 1968 in France and the UK it seemed possible to aspire to universities that would provide a wide variety of educational possibilities, although with smaller numbers than now. I will show in Chap. 6 how far that idea of wide possibilities was from being realised in the USA.

Here and now in the UK, it is instructive to reconsider the reality of those optimistic times of hope and innocence on campus. Peering back from 2023, they seem to hold the first signs of how left and right of the political spectrum began gradually hollowing out the power and potency of the language we can use on campus, not to mention the quality of our thought, and the integrity of our identities. The campus universe has been gradually shrinking—or rather, been shrunk. And so insidiously, that we on campus have only recently accepted the need to address the shocking, intellectually impoverishing results that have been forced upon us.

Whereas the democratic deficit in 1968 reflected student naivety about participation in university education, today's deficit pertains to the sense of reduced independence of the education system and inadequate engagement by students and academics to hold politicians to account. The unsolvable tension for capitalist nation states is that, while independence of education is in principle a requirement for liberal democracy, it is also the implicit antithesis of capitalist states' rationale—to extract the maximum possible economic productivity from its citizens. In effect, the state withdraws except to create the conditions of a labour and knowledge market.

2.2 Ricœur's Idea of the University

Ricœur's interest in and active engagement with university life dates from well before 1968. From 1947 onwards he was thinking reflectively and critically about the university sector and became engaged fully with campus life as an academic with a considerable teaching load which he relished, first at Strasbourg (1950–1956), then at Paris Sorbonne and Paris Nanterre (1956–1970). Ricœur's experiences on the Nanterre campus is spanned by four essays, one from 1964, two from 1968, and one from 1971 (Ricœur 1964; 1968a, b; 1971).

In his 1964 essay *Faire l'Université* (*Making the University*), Ricœur predicted that student unrest was a situation with wider societal implications, and had proposed some solutions which Dosse analysed in *Paul Ricœur: les sens d'une vie* (*The Many Meanings of One Life*) (Dosse 2000, 465–466). Ricœur's arguments therein are similar to those discussed fifty years later by Sperlinger, MacLellan and Pettigrew in their 2018 book *Who are universities for?* They show how, although the student population has expanded greatly since Ricœur's recommendations for reform, other policies and many universities remain persistently deficient in several ways. They, like him, criticize the exclusive nature of universities: they see an urgent need to change and accept nonstandard candidates, even by circumventing normal application procedures if necessary, in order to secure equality amongst applicants. They recommend offering non-standard routes and consider the whole of a person's life as potentially open to university education (Sperlinger et al. 2018, 11).

Four years later, in the preface Ricœur wrote for *Conceptions de l'université (Designing the University)*, both his idealism and his pragmatic belief in the transformative power of the new project at Nanterre are evident. He reported upon interviews he had conducted to investigate students' views of university life. He argued that the grand liberal vision of meritocracy mostly for the elite that had hitherto animated the university was no longer viable, because the university needed to be egalitarian and to become a mass-intake venture that must focus both upon high level research and the provision of professional studies and technical training in preparation for the workplace (Ricœur 1968a, 9). Ricœur viewed this choice between technical or academic pathways as a positive development and embraced its more expansive vision. Some more recent commentators are less flexible—and also less consistent. For example, Collini, in his 2012 book *What are universities for?* criticises Cardinal John Henry Newman for elitism, but then himself presents a similar vision of exclusivist universities; Collini differentiates between training and education in a way that shows they must be kept separate—an approach that differs from Ricœur's desire for equality of opportunity and parity of provision for intellectual and vocational courses (Collini 2012, 48, 56).

Ricœur saw how those who represented the liberal ideal had become defensive and had begun to understand the struggles between liberal elitism (represented by academics) and radical militancy (represented by students) as dangerous for universities. The Paris intellectual scene was dominated at that time by Marxist thought, which he found strident and unproductive; he shared the non-Marxist belief that when militant activism by students begins to dominate the liberal university, this weakens the university considerably because the radical vision comprises socialist, even Marxist thinking that—in his view—was not related to intellectual understanding. Student activism manifested itself in the students demanding recognition of their intellectual, social and sexual needs (such as boys demanding access to girls' dormitories—the girls' views are not known); Ricœur was unconvinced as to whether such *recognition* of student needs by university authorities would in fact lead to increased student *participation* in university life (Ricœur 1968a, 16–18).

In response, he proposed three urgent moves. First, to reformulate the idea of the liberal university so as to create a permeable membrane between the university and society which would help resist domination by what he construed as societal utilitarianism and forms of rebellion that are purely destructive. Second, using the Republican ideal of individual participation more openly, he wanted to insist upon full student participation in policymaking. He believed this to be both necessary and realistic, since involving students in implementing realistic policies would, he expected, also temper their excessive demands and challenge modern radical movements. Third, he hoped to challenge modern consumerist culture, so that the young would see the contrast between the ideas-based university and the market-driven world beyond the campus clearly, in the hope that this would help students create better communication between the university and the outside world. To help students appreciate the interdependent nature of their world, he also insisted upon interdisciplinarity, thereby also giving them greater curricular choice (Ricœur 1968a, 19–21).

Responding to increased tension, Ricœur wrote *Réforme et révolution dans l'Université* (*Reform and Revolution in the University*) in what seemed then like the full heat of the student revolts: it was first published in *Le Monde* in June 1968 in three parts (on the 9th, 11th and 12th) when the rioting was intense, and the Sorbonne was under occupation, thus providing his responses 'in real time' to what was going on in Paris campuses and in other locations in France (Ricœur 1968b). His proposed solution was to include more democratic processes that directly engaged students. This was Ricœur in action: seeking to temper frustrations with the pragmatic need to be conciliatory during an ongoing crisis for the university sector and for society generally. As a result of the riots, students won the right to sit on management committees (*cogestion* = co-management); however, as Ricœur had presciently warned in 1964, it turned out to be a somewhat illusory victory because committee bureaucracy slowed down innovation: students often did not witness the changes they initiated (Ricœur 1964). The 1968 débacle provides a filter for Ricœur's evolving views on universities, and in 1971—still raw about Nanterre, his resignation and failure to realise his dream (see Sect. 5.2)—he wrote a preface about his philosophy for *Hermeneutic phenomenology: the philosophy of Paul Ricœur*: it throws contemporary thought from that time in the UK and across Europe and many other areas into sharp relief (Ricœur 1971). After all the hectic violence of '68, he places the written text at the centre of human development which becomes the 'place for the decentering and dispossession of immediacy'; he hopes that 'meaning comes to the ego through the power of the word' as a way to balance his 'permanent mistrust of the pretensions of the subject in posing itself as the foundation of its own meaning' (Ricœur 1971, xv). With this stance, Ricœur gives an early version of his model of the self: individual agency is both autonomous and ego driven, and yet also situated as a self-reflexive critique about its own shortcomings. This is not what happened in his dealings with rebellious students on the Nanterre campus, whose excitement about their moral and political freedom led them to reject discussion, negotiation and conciliation. Nor does it work now, with the opposite student response of intense state-authorized aggressions about race and discrimination that lead students and staff to disengage from possible controversy.

2.3 Discrimination on Campus

Intense discrimination against Muslims on UK campuses is currently being driven by the government's counterextremism policy, Prevent, which successfully creates suspicion of Muslim students and staff in public places such as schools, hospitals and universities (Holmwood and Aitlhadj 2023; Aked 2020; Guest et al. 2020). Prevent is part of an arsenal of techniques adopted by successive UK governments to create 'an enemy within'; such techniques purportedly create 'harmony' in nation-states, at the cost of state-authorised civilian surveillance of Muslims and their thoughts and discourse. Empirical evidence from UK universities shows that both students and staff make explicit connections between counterterror surveillance and suppression of free speech (Scott-Baumann et al. 2020; Scott-Baumann and Perfect 2021). The ways in which the identities of British Muslims are depicted differently and in discriminatory polemical security rhetoric are also discussed by Khadijah Elshayyal in *Muslim Identity Politics: Islam, Activism and Equality in Britain* (Elshayyal 2018). The 'enemy within' concept originated in its modern iteration with Carl Schmitt, a political theorist who believed that this was the way to create a stable peaceful state (Schmitt 1988).

The chilling of speech is particularly pronounced in universities with a significant minority of Muslim students. The Charity Commission has active oversight of student unions, which are charities, and it has actively supported Prevent restrictions in intrusive ways, to purportedly prevent *jihadism* on campus (Scott-Baumann and Perfect 2021). Such intrusions, however, are unjustified: UK campuses host over 2 million students each year, and the BBC database of 276 British jihadists categorizes 13 as 'extremist students'; yet only 6 of them were members of British universities, and there may not even be any correlation between their choices and their having been on campus (BBC News 2017). Nevertheless, in attempting to avoid unjust and disproportionate vilification, Muslim students report that they often decide to avoid censure by self-censoring their own views on a wide range of important topics in the classroom and outside of it (e.g. Islam, UK foreign policy, western feminism and counterterror measures). They may also desist from inviting speakers considered by non-Muslims to be socially conservative, who in turn may self-censor on these topics if an invitation to speak does transpire (Scott-Baumann et al. 2020). This 'chilling' contrasts with Ricœur's vision of the student having ready access to open debate with academic staff. Crude 'othering' of Muslims along the 'enemy within' lines is a recurrent theme in this book as it forms such an important part of Western culture—contemporary and historical—and the idea of the university.

2.4 Discrimination Against Colour

There also appears to be a strong element of anti-blackness in some government behaviour. The government denies structural racism, as demonstrated in the 2021 *Commission on Race and Ethnic Disparities* (Commission on Race and Ethnic Disparities 2021). Anti-racist voices are raised in shock at such denial but find themselves less supported than they should be by a university sector concerned about how to express itself appropriately, and which thus often keeps quiet (Woolley 2021; Mohdin et al. 2021). This eviscerating process ensures compliance through the suppression of different, potentially dissenting voices in the university community: such voices may often be from people of colour, non-aligned politically, non-heteronormative and young, and their demands can lead to suppression of white voices raised in their support. At the same time, Elshayyal critiques the fear of identity politics as a fissiparous impulse that leads groups away from the national interest; rather, she celebrates the importance of group identity (Elshayyal 2018). Also germane here as a distorted identity politics is 'the great replacement theory', which is the thesis that people of colour are taking over the white western world; its promulgators—Eric Kaufmann and others—work with think tanks like Policy Exchange that influence government, and target those who see themselves as integrated into white culture and aligned with the current political establishment (Kaufmann 2018).

2.5 The Culture Wars and Wokeness

The 'chilling' effect has been created by a toxic amalgamation of counterterror policies and the phenomenon known as 'culture wars'. Whilst the term can be traced to the 1960s American civil rights movement, in the 1990s, culture wars was used by the American sociologist James Davison Hunter to describe a USA movement that believed it was fighting for the essence of America by using binaries to assert rights and wrongs in a polarizing way. In the US it is demonstrated by the polarization between black and white populations. Here in the current British context, culture wars can be seen as a form of cultural nationalism, manifested in the battle of words between libertarian right wing and no-platforming left wing voices. In this context, it becomes imperative that each saves values and historical memories from distortion by the other. Yet, in the UK there is some doubt in the public's mind about whether a culture war exists, and, if it does, whether it is as significant a problem as the media asserts (Duffy et al. 2021). For it seems to be the case that the media augments public belief in such wars by increasingly writing about them: whilst it was mentioned 178 times in media conversations in 2019, in 2020 534 articles referred to it, and in 2021 1470 articles discussed it; accordingly, there was a 'a significant increase in public belief that the UK is divided by culture wars' (Duffy et al. 2021). Yet the research also found that:

> Those from a minority ethnic background (61%) are much less likely than white people (81%) to feel the UK is divided in general. And since 2020, the proportion who hold this view has grown slightly among white people, while declining slightly among people from ethnic minorities. (Duffy et al. 2022, 4)

These data raise a very interesting question: why would white people feel more convinced by the idea of culture wars than global majority people living as minorities in the UK, when it is global majority people who have suffered the effects of much worse for centuries? This may be (partially) explained by the ineffable structural characteristics of surveys: the wording of questions and the sequencing of topics can have unpredictable effects, no matter the level of care taken in the architecture of the survey. However, it may be also worth considering that we are witnessing the bitter harvest of 'the great replacement theory' (Kaufmann 2018). If it is this thesis that is at the heart of the culture wars, then, by virtue of its targeted nature, it *will* impress itself more upon white populations than upon those of colour; by contrast, the latter appreciate the paradox that whilst they are in the majority globally, they have not had the power, status, finances and social mobility that mostly white populations enjoy. The class of the privileged, as a form of identity, resists any pressure to share its gains in terms of what and who and how it knows, fearing downward mobility (Goldthorpe 2016). To frame it in Ricœurian imagery, 'contemporary thought feeds itself on the debris of this clash' (Ricœur 1971) between 'left' and 'right', so that perceived gains on one side (the left via Black Lives Matter) lead to increased activity on the other (the right via 'great replacement theory' protagonists).

Numerous writers have documented the imbalance and discrimination that face those of colour and those visibly identifiable as different from the 'white norm': in *Why I'm No Longer Talking to White People about Race*, Eddo-Lodge provides an overview which includes an analysis of the racist murder of Stephen Lawrence in 1993 (Eddo-Lodge 2018); in *In Black and White*, Alexandra Wilson, who felt compelled to become a junior barrister following the fatal stabbing of her family friend on his way home, explores the institutionalized racism of the justice system (Wilson 2021); and Isabel Wilkerson's exploration of American racism through the prism of 'eight pillars of caste' is very perceptive in understanding the cruel logic behind racial dehumanisation (Wilkerson 2023). In universities too my research team and I uncovered systemic discrimination as well as the considerable difficulties involved in attempts to be heard without prejudice and misunderstanding (Scott-Baumann et al. 2020). Working to counteract the reductive counterterror programme Prevent, our *Islam on campus* researchers wrote in 2020 that the team:

> approaches radicalization not as a personal process of identity change, but as a discursive category operant within higher education settings that refracts broader anxieties about risk and risky identities. (Scott-Baumann et al. 2020, 147)

A characteristic of the culture wars is the use of denigratory terms to both mock and ensure polarization, for example, through accusations of 'wokeness'. 'Woke', according to the Oxford English Dictionary research team, is a term that has been known anecdotally for many years. In the early 1960s, it denoted being well-informed in the context of black communities in Harlem, Chicago and elsewhere in the USA, implying perhaps being well informed about race and discrimination. This meaning is now contained explicitly in its current OED definition: 'alert to racial or social discrimination and injustice; frequently in "stay woke"'. Yet articles in the libertarian online journal *Spiked*,[2] Andrew Doyle in *Free Speech And Why It Matters* (Doyle 2021), and many others in the social media world use their various platforms loudly to define 'woke' and 'wokeness' as a sinister force, describing it as an attempt to stop people speaking freely, in case they offend someone, with truth-speaking held up as the inevitable victim. I believe it is urgently necessary to challenge and replace this commonly held misconception that discrimination is an illusion created by 'lefties' who are too 'woke', thereby fostering the culture wars. For example, in *Counter Wokecraft*, Pincourt and Lindsay present university campus life as a

---

[2] https://www.spiked-online.com.

dystopia of communities falsely separated by 'woke' academics into the privileged and the oppressed (Pincourt and Lindsay 2021). They see critical race theory as the ideological contaminant of natural and normal societal structures: they reject CRT's assertion that we must understand the modern world as shaped by white supremacy, and also the urgent need to focus on racism, sexism and other forms of structural discrimination. Such polemical views are challenged by authors such as Gavan Titley who, in *Is Free Speech Racist?*, attempts to depict a more balanced approach (Titley 2020). Eric Heinze presents a view based upon liberal democratic principles, proposing that free speech is the key to all our freedoms (Heinze 2017, 2022), whereas Yassir Morsi analyses the issue via his direct, personal experience in *Radical Skin, Moderate Masks* (Morsi 2017).

In this 'anti-woke' atmosphere, the British government has passed the Higher Education (Freedom of Speech) Act as a means to ostensibly abolish all constraints on discussion. This is a libertarian move designed to invite open abuse of anyone, including vulnerable minorities and to encourage more 'right wing' staff and students to speak out. We see this in the Minister of State for Higher and Further Education's letter in June 2022 to all vice chancellors recommending that they do not engage in diversity training as that will supposedly harm free speech (see Sect. 6.8).[3] This is an exemplification of an imbalance of power which, as Sallenave would describe it, is intended to protect talk from above and impose silence from below (Sallenave 2021); universities must fight it.

As part of the 'culture wars' the educational curriculum in Britain is currently under attack by both 'the left' and 'the right': the attack from 'the left' is about the curriculum's failure to take account of the enduring effects of the British Empire, centuries of slavery and the prominent remains of such abusive riches in civic society; 'the right's' attack rejects this in order to maintain conventional historical narratives and continue to tell the histories of the victors. Libertarian attacks take the form of mocking, ignoring, deceiving or gaslighting those minorities whom history has neither listened to nor allowed to speak; and they also pillory mercilessly those who speak for them, as Corinne Fowler was tormented when she spoke in her work on colonial legacies for the National Trust (Fowler 2021; Doward 2020); so attempts to tell the story of the colonised have borne patchy results—notwithstanding the cultural impact of David Olusoga, Akala, Afua Hirsch and others (Olusoga 2021; Akala 2019; Hirsch 2018).

Yet knowledge creation and knowledge absorption are vital for democracies and their ostensibly intellectually independent universities—and this process must include dissent: epistemological, political and social factors necessitate the freedom to disagree civilly and to share with others the risk we all run of offending each other. Ricœur applied his thought to specific aspects of an unjust world (Ricœur 2010), yet his work cannot provide the answers to why the world is so; thus, after the following section on Equality Diversity and Inclusion, I offer a radically different view from his—that of Wael Hallaq (see also Sect. 4.1). This sets the scene for the tension

---

[3] https://wonkhe.com/wp-content/wonkhe uploads/2022/06/Letter-Regarding-Free-Speech-and-External-Assurance-Schemes-1.pdf.

between Ricœur's powerful and transformative work on use of language, and the need to find a vehicle through which to disseminate his work in ways that allow us to address live injustices. This requires, as Ricœur recommends, taking the voice of the 'other' seriously; accordingly, these writers include females, people of colour and the non-religious, who would be silenced by the 'antiwoke'.

2.6 Endless Distraction and Inaction

Since the Equality Act 2010, Equality, Diversity and Inclusion (EDI) has been the policy adopted by both public and private organisations to reverse the chilling effect that minorities experience in their organisations; the strategy was to use open discussions to facilitate better understanding of unconscious bias, and reduce discrimination. In terms of reducing discrimination on grounds of religion, there has been little progress in support and understanding. In terms of reducing racism, Sana Ahsan, a clinical psychologist who argues for the 'dismantling of whiteness' in order to practice anti-racism, finds EDI initiatives ineffective; she thus proposes 'Endless Distraction and Inaction' as a more appropriate acronym (Ahsan 2022). Challenging negative difference on campus via the Equality, Diversity and Inclusion initiative has been sluggish. The university sector has had access for decades to data about chronic underachievement of global majority/UK minority students and lack of career progression for global majority/UK minority staff, yet EDI only gained a sense of priority in the wake of the murder of George Floyd in 2020 and the Black Lives Matter movement. In the UK, universities and medical schools are only now (in the 2020s) appointing EDI deans and instructing their staff to 'sort it out' as a matter of urgency. In the current atmosphere, EDI action is seen to be necessary; yet both left- and right-wing approaches to resolving discrimination (on grounds of difference and rewriting history, or by denying difference and decolonisation, respectively) are experiencing difficulties. As Ricœur reflects, overcoming these difficulties and struggles requires the successful management of negative emotions:

> What natural right does not recognise is the place of struggle in the conquest of equality and justice, the role of negative conduct in the motivation leading to struggle: lack of consideration, humiliation, disdain, to say nothing of violence in all its physical and psychological forms. (Ricœur 2016, 3:293)

Moreover, even though universities are surely the best placed to resolve the culture wars through reasoned analysis and discussion, they are accused of fomenting them. This has led to more caution and less open discussion. In 2022, the public felt unsure about whether university academics should be free to say what they want (32%) or be careful not to cause offence (34%) (Duffy et al. 2022, 19). This confusion has led to sector-wide chilling effects that influence academic staff and their curricula, as well as student activism: we witness balanced, evidence-based and rich discussions of colonial damage, exploitation of natural resources, foreign policy and racism all falling prey to a so-called culture war. This is paradoxical as the methods of the traditionalists seem modern (brave libertarian free speech) and the methods of the modernisers seem regressive (oppressive no-platforming). Identity, race and religion (especially Islam) feature prominently because they are especially apt for presenting disorientating and contradictory versions of reality—a trick borrowed from authoritarian populism and applied to issues of culture such as statues and the university curriculum.

2.7 Wael Hallaq

The university must maintain a critical voice independent of the state apparatus and this is discussed and supported in *Restating Orientalism*, Wael Hallaq's sweeping critique of the modern university. Hallaq, who is not Muslim, brings Islamic scholarship to this analysis; he understands the university to be the subjectivised 'elite pedagogical machine of the state' (Hallaq 2018, 104), and accuses the university sector of creating severe moral damage. As the locus of 'all branches of Western learning—the sciences, professional studies, social sciences, and humanities', Hallaq holds the university responsible (along with 'the totality of Western political, economic, and cultural structures that sustain these forms of knowledge') for the existential crisis facing humanity and its environmental habitat (Moin 2019; Hallaq 2018). This is an extreme position, yet clearly an alternative paradigm is required to return universities to some form of autonomy, and in his ground-breaking *The Impossible State*, Hallaq expounds on the moral central paradigm of pre-modern Shari'a, and proposes, through education, the cultivation of ethico-political subjects to resolve the crises of modernity (Hallaq 2013).

Hallaq also argues that, contra pre-modern governance, the bureaucratic machinery of the modern state is such that it develops its own type of community, with the result that the bureaucracy becomes the state. In his chapter *The Political Paradox* Ricœur discusses this phenomenon as the way in which—as states become more rational—they also create more opportunities for the perversion of such increased rationality (Ricœur 1965, 247–270). He saw this in Budapest, Algeria and with other political events. Yet, at that point in the 1950s and early 1960s he still believed that the university could provide the necessary lead for improving such moral failures. After all, it was Hungarian university students who initiated the revolution against Soviet domination in 1956. It would seem, however, that Ricœur's optimism was unfounded: Mike Higton (2013) is damning in documenting 'what he sees as the virtual collapse of the Humboldtian vision of a university as a coherent community of seekers after public truth' (cited in Murad 2020, 237).

More positively, and contra Hallaq, I propose that it is precisely because the university *does* constitute a different sort of community (despite its much-weakened state), that it *still* poses such a threat to the nation state's bureaucratic community. This is also precisely why the university must continue to strive for academic freedom and balanced discursive free speech, and to re-strengthen its understanding of itself as a community of inquiry and ideas and a community of individuals who work together to actively consider a better world. *This* is where the university can transform society by guiding students in discussion and insisting upon both the university's autonomy and its integrity within the modern state.

2.8 Secularism and Islam

In *Critique and Conviction* Ricœur was critical of the French state's rigid adherence to *laïcité* (secularism) and he was in favour of allowing the Muslim veil in schools, forbidden by French law (Ricœur et al. 1998). He saw how French secularism reacts to Islam, based upon anticlericalism, while in fact being firmly grounded in retained Catholic traditions such as the timing and naming of holidays in the church calendar. This post-colonial approach forces Muslim French schoolgirls into impossible choices that are unethical and wilfully imposed by the French state. Less philosophically and more sociologically, in *Critique and Conviction* he challenged the detrimental effect of *laïcité* upon Muslim girls' and women's education (Ricœur et al. 1998, 135; Scott-Baumann 2011). Over several decades, Ricœur wrote often about this French Catholic form of secularism, born out of virulent revolutionary anti-clerical fervour and a French form of socialism.[4]

In the UK, contemporary British Muslim theologian Shuruq Naguib has been debating the tension between the way in which the modern campus insists that secularism is a neutral position, and the current hierarchies of power and knowledge in the Islamic Studies field, which tends to be male dominated (see Sect. 5.5). In her analysis, this creates both a complex overarching democratic deficit issue that is perpetuated by male gendered discourses, and an intellectual issue regarding academic parity (or otherwise) between religious and secular voices in a democracy.

Naguib also considers the textual hierarchy embedded in Islamic Studies teaching, which can habituate students into a pedagogy that is based on positivist and sceptical historical approaches, when taught according to Western scholarship. She notes that an approach more inflected towards revelation when taught according to Islamic scholarship is much less encouraged. Naguib believes and hopes that there will soon be a gradual confluence between these two approaches, and that the academy will be able to work closely with faith-based Islamic colleges (Scott-Baumann et al. 2020, Chap. 8). Currently, in England and Scotland only 20 universities teach Islamic Studies to any depth and the majority focus exclusively on Sunni Islam (Scott-Baumann et al. 2020). Most of the comments in my work are about Sunni Islam, as the most numerous grouping and because Shi'i Islam was experienced to a lesser extent in Europe (Scharbrodt and Shanneik 2020). Furthermore, modern Shi'ism often found itself reactive to Sunni Islam, partly due to lack of Shi'i resources compared with those of Sunni Islam. With the 1979 Iranian Revolution, scholars became motivated to consider Shi'ism on its own terms and new work is now constantly developing on Shi'i

---

[4] This can be seen in Stewart and Bien's anthology of his early work, covering 1956–1973 (Ricœur 1974).

2.8 Secularism and Islam

religious scholarship, ethnographies of lived experience and increased commitment to histories, to devotional practices and, above all, the ways in which such work can help explain Shi'ism to the modern world (Esposti and Scott-Baumann 2019). The university sector is actually well-placed to improve the quality of conversation around and between Sunni and Shi'i Islam.

Habermas has also been thinking about this and attempts to contextualise critical reflection and engagement (the latter formulated as praxis) more broadly within proposed implementation of two important features of a functioning democracy: constitutional patriotism and observance of a public space in which important matters can be debated (Habermas et al. 2003). A pluralistic liberal democratic constitution is the necessary underpinning for his vision of the future, characterised by group identity that goes beyond ethno-cultural identification and religion, in order that individuals can come together in the public sphere on equal terms. I return to this issue in Chap. 7, with a German example of polity praxis.

I suggest we are being deprived of opportunities to discuss and solve societal problems together with those of different belief systems, and I propose that to do this at university we must also be able to call upon historical precedents. It is therefore important to appreciate the interwoven historical connections between Islam and the West in modes of communication, now shared by the university tradition. The world's oldest degree-granting universities were Islamic and catered for both men and women; in fact, the first, *Al-Qarawiyyin*, developed out of a mosque-madrasa complex that was founded in 859 by a woman, Fatima al-Fihri (Das 2021). In those early centuries of Islamic empire, Islamicate scholars translated Greek dialectical works into Arabic and Muslims developed and deployed the *Kalām*-philosophical method of argumentation in their theological dialectical debates.[5] The diffusion of Greek dialectics into Muslim argumentative discourse was first utilised by the Mu'tazilites (rationalistic theologians)[6] during early Abbasid rule (750–900), and later adopted by all *kalām* schools.[7] The existing 'proto-system of argumentation' was developed into 'a specific style that involved a methodological question and answer format with use and emphasis on language and logic' and argumentation became a public art form (Taşköprüzāde 2020, 22–23). In the following centuries, this science became 'embedded within the educational curricula [Dars-i Niẓāmī][8]

---

[5] See Taşköprüzāde (2020, 153–154, and 198–203) for the various fundamental differences between the Qur'anic and *Kalām*-philosophical methods of disputation.

[6] The content of Mu'tazilism (rationalistic theology) was philosophical theology, and its method dialectic disputation (Gutas 1998, 161).

[7] *Kalām* can be understood as 'dialectical theology using a dialectical method (*jadal*) of reasoning for apologetics' (Taşköprüzāde 2020, 162). Early Islamic *kalām* debates were about the creed and certain divisive issues, such as free will, predestination, and the imamate (Walbridge 2019, 88–89). For an overview of *kalām* schools see Dāmād (2015), and Ziai (2008).

[8] Dating back to the thirteenth century, Niẓām al-Dīn's curriculum, 'stressed dialectical skills […] and was designed to 'teach the student how to understand texts through a deep knowledge of logic, the inner workings of language, and rhetoric. nineteenth and twentieth century Muslim reformers partially supplanted the Dars-i Niẓāmī by putting 'more stress on primary religious texts and less on logic' (Walbridge 2019, 84–85).

and its perceived superiority over dialectics [...] established' (Taşköprüzāde 2020, 24).

The intertwined roots of traditional communication evidenced here between Islam and the products of ancient Greek culture (both integral to western civilizations) show how impossible it is to justify the secular state's assertions that it is liberal and neutral. The secular state is a complex confection of centuries of culture, religion and ideologies from many civilisations. Accordingly, Habermas would like to offer more equal acceptance for faith-based thought, and considers whether religious citizens are forced to shoulder an excessive, asymmetric burden because they have to translate their political arguments into secular language that is (assumed to be) neutral and accessible to all; he argues that religious reasoning *should* be permitted in public debate, albeit not within formal political institutions like parliaments, which seem to remove democratic voice from the religious (Habermas 2006).

Universities are plagued with huge issues about funding, about subject coverage (STEM taking precedence) and even about examination regimes and what counts as cheating and plagiarism, as well as what 'truth' might look like. As Ricoeur predicted, these problems are those of society as well. Faced with these problems that truly threaten the identity and purpose of the university, I agree with Steven Jones that overly bureaucratized university management systems have clearly failed to accept the challenge to develop into an active, independent component of a nation's cultural life (Jones 2022), and thus, seventy years after Ricœur's original concerns that the university was not fit for purpose, we need to really take democracy seriously and interact actively with government and policymakers as necessary interlocutors with faith-based arguments and otherwise.

References

Ahsan, Sana. 2022. "EDI": Endless Distraction and Inaction. *The Psychologist* 35: 22–27.
Akala. 2019. *Natives: Race and Class in the Ruins of Empire*. London: Two Roads.
Bulaitis, Zoe Hope. 2021. '"Minimum Expectations" Are No Way to Value the Arts, Humanities, and Social Sciences'. *Impact of Social Sciences* (blog). 7 June 2021. https://blogs.lse.ac.uk/impactofsocialsciences/2021/06/07/minimum-expectations-are-no-way-to-value-the-arts-humanities-and-social-sciences/.
Collini, Stefan. 2012. *What Are Universities For?* London: Penguin.
Commission on Race and Ethnic Disparities. 2021. 'The Report of the Commission on Race and Ethnic Disparities'. Independent. London: Commission on Race and Ethnic Disparities. https://www.gov.uk/government/publications/the-report-of-the-commission-on-race-and-ethnic-disparities.
Dāmād, Muṣṭafā Muḥaqqiq. 2015. 'The Quran and Schools of Islamic Theology and Philosophy'. In *The Study Quran: A New Translation and Commentary*. Eds. Seyyed Hossein Nasr, Caner K. Dagli, Maria Massi Dakake, and Joseph B. Lumbard. Translated by Seyyed Hossein Nasr, 1st edition, 1719–35. New York, NY: HarperOne, an imprint of Collins Publishers.
Das, Bidisha. 2021. 'These Are the World's 11 Oldest, Awe-Inspiring Universities'. News. *The College Post* (blog). 26 February 2021. https://thecollegepost.com/oldest-universities/.

References

Davies, William. 2022. 'How Many Words Does It Take to Make a Mistake?' *London Review of Books*, 24 February 2022. https://www.lrb.co.uk/the-paper/v44/n04/william-davies/how-many-words-does-it-take-to-make-a-mistake.

Dosse, François. 2000. *Paul Ricœur: Les sens d'une vie*. Paris: La Découverte.

Doward, Jamie. 2020. I've Been Unfairly Targeted, Says Academic at Heart of National Trust "woke" Row. *The Observer*, 20 December 2020, sec. UK news. https://www.theguardian.com/uk-news/2020/dec/20/ive-been-unfairly-targeted-says-academic-at-heart-of-national-trust-woke-row.

Doyle, Andrew. 2021. *Free Speech And Why It Matters*. London: Constable.

Duffy, Bobby, Kirstie Hewlett, George Murkin, Rebecca Benson, Rachel Hesketh, Ben Page, Gideon Skinner, and Glenn Gottfried. 2021. Culture Wars in the UK: How the Public Understand the Debate. Culture Wars in the UK. King's College, London: The Policy Institute; Ipsos MORI. https://www.kcl.ac.uk/policy-institute/assets/culture-wars-in-the-uk-how-the-public-understand-the-debate.pdf.

Duffy, Bobby, Paul Stoneman, Kirstie Hewlett, George May, Gideon Skinner, and Glenn Gottfried. 2022. Freedom of Speech in the UK's "Culture War". London: King's College London. https://www.kcl.ac.uk/policy-institute/assets/freedom-of-speech-in-the-uks-culture-war.pdf.

Eddo-Lodge, Reni. 2018. *Why I'm No Longer Talking to White People about Race*. London: Bloomsbury.

Esposti, Emanuelle Degli, and Alison Scott-Baumann. 2019. 'Fighting for "Justice", Engaging the Other: Shi'a Muslim Activism on the British University Campus'. *Religions* 10 (3): 189. https://doi.org/10.3390/rel10030189.

Goldthorpe, J. 2016. Social class mobility in modern Britain: changing structure, constant process. *Journal of the British Academy* 4: 89–111. https://doi.org/10.5871/jba/004.089.

Gutas, Dimitri. 1998. *Greek Thought, Arabic Culture*. Routledge. http://www.myilibrary.com?id=281629.

Habermas, Jürgen. 2006. Religion in the Public Sphere. *European Journal of Philosophy* 14 (1): 1–25. https://doi.org/10.1111/j.1468-0378.2006.00241.x.

Habermas, Jürgen, Jacques Derrida, and Giovanna Borradori. 2003. *Philosophy in a Time of Terror: Dialogues with Jürgen Habermas and Jacques Derrida*. Chicago; London: University of Chicago Press.

Hallaq, Wael B. 2013. *The Impossible State: Islam, Politics, and Modernity's Moral Predicament*. New York: Columbia University Press.

Hallaq, Wael B. 2018. *Restating Orientalism: A Critique of Modern Knowledge*. New York: Columbia University Press.

Heinze, Eric. 2017. *Hate Speech and Democratic Citizenship*, 1st ed. Oxford: Oxford University Press.

Heinze, Eric. 2022. *The Most Human Right: Why Free Speech Is Everything*. Cambridge, Massachusetts; London, England: The MIT Press.

Higton, Mike. 2013. *A Theology of Higher Education*. Oxford: Oxford Univ. Press.

Hirsch, Afua. 2018. *Brit(ish): On Race, Identity and Belonging*. Illustrated. London: Vintage.

Johnson, Paul. 2020. 'Too Many Students Take Courses That Don't Benefit Them or the Economy'. *The Times*, 2 March 2020. https://ifs.org.uk/publications/14741.

Jones, Steven. 2022. *Universities Under Fire: Hostile Discourses and Integrity Deficits in Higher Education*. S.l.: Springer Nature.

Kaufmann, Eric. 2018. *Whiteshift: Populism*. Immigration and the Future of White Majorities: Penguin.

Mohdin, Aamna, Peter Walker, and Nazia Parveen. 2021. 'No 10's Race Report Widely Condemned as "Divisive"'. *The Guardian*, 31 March 2021, sec. World news. https://www.theguardian.com/world/2021/mar/31/deeply-cynical-no-10-report-criticises-use-of-institutional-racism.

Moin, Azfar. 2019. Moin on Hallaq, "Restating Orientalism: A Critique of Modern Knowledge". *Humanities and Social Sciences Online*, H-Asia, December. https://networks.h-net.org/node/22055/reviews/5542145/moin-hallaq-restating-orientalism-critique-modern-knowledge.

Morsi, Yassir. 2017. *Radical Skin, Moderate Masks: De-Radicalising the Muslim and Racism in Post-Racial Societies*. Maryland, US; London, UK: Rowman & Littlefield.
Murad, Abdal Hakim. 2020. *Travelling Home: Essays on Islam in Europe*. Quilliam Press Ltd.
Olusoga, David. 2021. *Black and British: A Forgotten History*. New Edit/Cover edition. London: Picador.
Palfreyman, David, and Paul Temple. 2017. *Universities and Colleges: A Very Short Introduction*.
Pincourt, Charles, and James Lindsay. 2021. *Counter Wokecraft: A Field Manual for Combatting the Woke in the University and Beyond*. Orlando, Florida: New Discourses.
Ricœur, Paul. 1964. Faire l'Université. *Esprit* 328 (5–6): 1162–1172.
Ricœur, Paul. 1965. *History and Truth: Translated with an Introduction by Charles A. Kelbley*. Translated by Charles A. Kelbey. 2nd ed. Evanston, IL: Northwestern University Press.
Ricœur, Paul. 1968a. 'Preface'. In *Conceptions de l'université. Jacques Dreże and Jean Debelle*, 8–22. Paris: Éditions Universitaires.
Ricœur, Paul. 1968b. Réforme et Révolution Dans l'Université. *Esprit*, 372 (6/7): 987–1002.
Ricœur, Paul. 1971. 'Preface'. In *Hermeneutic Phenomenology: The Philosophy of Paul Ricœur. Don Ihde.*, xiii–xvii. Evanston: Northwestern University Press.
Ricœur, Paul. 2010. 'Being a Stranger'. Translated by Alison Scott-Baumann. *Theory, Culture and Society* 27 (5): 37–48.
Ricœur, Paul. 2016. *Philosophical Anthropology*. Edited by Johann Michel and Jerome Poree. Translated by David Pellauer. Vol. 3. 3 vols. Writings and Lectures. Cambridge, UK; Malden, MA: Polity Press.
Ricœur, Paul, François Azouvi, and Marc de Launay. 1998. *Critique and Conviction: Conversations with François Azouvi and Marc de Launay*. Cambridge: Polity.
Sallenave, Danièle. 2021. *Parole en haut, silence en bas*. Tracts (Paris. 2019). Paris: Gallimard.
Scott-Baumann, Alison, Sariya Cheruvallil-Contractor, Shuruq Naguib, Mathew Guest, and Aisha Phoenix. 2020. *Islam on Campus: Contested Identities and the Cultures of Higher Education in Britain*. OUP Oxford.
Scott-Baumann, Alison, and Simon Perfect. 2021. *Freedom of Speech in Universities Islam, Charities and Counter-Terrorism*. Islam in the World. London & New York: Routledge, Taylor & Francis Group.
Scharbrodt, O., and Shanneik, Y, eds. 2020. *Shi'a Minorities in the Contemporary World: Migration, Transnationalism and Multilocality*. Edinburgh: Edinburgh University Press. p. 344.
Sperlinger, Tom, Josie McLellan, and Richard Pettigrew. 2018. *Who Are Universities for? Re-Making Higher Education*.
Taşköprüzāde, Aḥmad Khalīl. 2020. *A Treatise on Disputation and Argument*. Translated by Safaruk Z. Chowdhury. 1st ed. London: Dar al-Nicosia.
Titley, Gavan. 2020. *Is Free Speech Racist?* 1st ed. Debating Race. Cambridge, UK ; Medford, MA: Polity.
Townend, Judith. 2017. 'Freedom of Expression and the Chilling Effect'. In *The Routledge Companion to Media and Human Rights*, edited by Howard Tumber and Silvio Waisbord, 1st ed. London: Routledge. https://doi.org/10.4324/9781315619835.
Walbridge, John. 2019. 'The Islamic Art of Asking Questions'. *Renovatio: How Do We Know?* 3 (1): 83–92.
Wilson, Alexandra. 2021. *In Black and White: A Young Barrister's Story of Race and Class in a Broken Justice System*. London: Endeavour.
Woolley, Simon. 2021. 'Despite the Sewell Report, No 10 Can No Longer Remain in Denial about Racism'. *The Guardian*, 1 April 2021, sec. Opinion. https://www.theguardian.com/commentisfree/2021/apr/01/sewell-report-no-10-racism-protests.
Ziai, Hossein. 2008. 'Islamic Philosophy (Falsafa)'. In *The Cambridge Companion to Classical Islamic Theology*. 1st ed, ed. Tim Winter, 55–76. Cambridge: Cambridge University Press.

References

Open Access This chapter is licensed under the terms of the Creative Commons Attribution 4.0 International License (http://creativecommons.org/licenses/by/4.0/), which permits use, sharing, adaptation, distribution and reproduction in any medium or format, as long as you give appropriate credit to the original author(s) and the source, provide a link to the Creative Commons license and indicate if changes were made.

The images or other third party material in this chapter are included in the chapter's Creative Commons license, unless indicated otherwise in a credit line to the material. If material is not included in the chapter's Creative Commons license and your intended use is not permitted by statutory regulation or exceeds the permitted use, you will need to obtain permission directly from the copyright holder.

Chapter 3
Communities of Inquiry

Abstract Before diving into Ricœur's historical and conceptual experiences of free speech about Algeria, Nanterre and USA in Chaps. 4, 5 and 6, I provide in this chapter a clear working definition of 'free speech' as a negotiated process and explore how, by using the *Communities of Inquiry* approach, young people can learn the art of discussion as they progress through university. As an antidote to the chilling effects of the culture wars, this develops a politics of pedagogy that entails mutual recognition of each other's arguments and helps us to share the risk with each other of causing offence. There are significant differences between this approach and the communicational ethics of Habermas. This chapter and Chaps. 4 and 6 end with sample *Communities of Inquiry*.

Keywords *Communities of Inquiry* · Procedural ethics · Rhetoric · Addams · Allen · Habermas · Kant

3.1 Communicating and Acting

It is a human need to communicate our humanity to others and respond to them. Yet there is currently much tension in society that militates against open and productive conversation. Across universities in the UK, there are topics which have become so contentious that students and staff, in their own groups or mixed, have reached an impasse in communication, to the point that mediation is required, but is usually not forthcoming. Copious analyses are written about the free speech debate, but without practical solutions. Language, the instrument of mediation, is what Ricœur worked extensively on throughout his career, developing a philosophy that entails being linguistically active and taking responsibility, by being accountable for the way we express ourselves.

Whilst Immanuel Kant's morality was not dependent upon developing conversational bonds, Ricœur understood that our use of language to really try and communicate should be interpreted as a serious assertion of our personal moral position. He believed that the way we use and experience language will affect us and change us. This became integrated into his analysis of narrative: language never exists for its own sake; it must always pursue an attempt to reflect the experience of living in the world. Attendant upon this approach is his 'vehement insistence on preventing language from closing up on itself' (Ricœur 1991b, 19). This is as necessary offline, as it is online in the digital world—which Ricœur did not live to see in its current intensity. Online activism, Emma Dabiri observes, has become a performative device that bypasses real action and devalues language:

> We seem to have replaced *doing anything* with *saying something*, in a space where the word 'conversation' has achieved an obscenely inflated importance as a substitute for action. (Dabiri 2021, 11)

But of even greater interest, perhaps, is the offline trend on campus towards extreme caution in *both* conversation and action. I will show how this caution is manifest in students and also in free speech commentators. With regard to students, in 2016, 37% of students polled (in an online survey by the Higher Education Policy Institute (HEPI)) agreed that students should be 'protected from discrimination rather than allow unlimited free speech'; but in 2022 students agreeing with the same statement increased significantly to 61% (Hillman 2022, 4). Hillman concludes that 'the level of student support for greater restrictions on free expression is so high that it is unlikely to be something that higher education institutions can grapple with on their own, assuming it is thought to need tackling, but instead is an issue for wider society' (Hillman 2022, 14). I see this differently: the HEPI question offers two extreme alternatives, but surely protection from discrimination *should* be a (if not *the*) major priority at universities in order to make open debate possible. This finding demonstrates that students' awareness is consistent with that of the Equality Act in seeking to be careful about 'unlimited free speech' and I explore how to achieve that in this chapter.

3.2 Challenging the Curriculum on Discrimination

The university curriculum is itself a site of judgement. To take an example from philosophy, the curriculum accords much attention to Immanuel Kant. For Kant, the modern university is integral to the modern state, because it is there that individuals learn critical reasoning skills that are morally based. Furthermore, Kant proposed a threefold version of moral universalism in which he considers tripartite human autonomy at the personal (individual), communitarian (group-based) and cosmopolitan (society-based) levels. These constitute progressively more expansive concentric circles of responsibility which we can see in my Matryoshka doll model (see Sect. 1.1). Ricœur noted how Kant has also influenced the thought of American legal scholar Rawls and German philosopher Habermas. Habermas and others have sought to remedy Kant's reliance upon logic even for practical reason, which Kant proposed as distinct from theoretical reasoning whilst following the same basic two-part structure, 'a priori' and 'a posteriori'. The former, 'a priori', comprises the conditions of possibility for every empirical argument deployed for addressing an issue, whilst the latter 'a posteriori' comprises all the possible non-evidence-based prejudices, desires, pleasures etc. that one may deploy. These two levels of reasoning (theoretical and practical) impel right action for rational agents.

People of colour, however, were excluded 'a priori' as Kant believed them not to be rational agents; they could not be contained within 'a priori' conditions of possibility. Accordingly, he saw the enterprise and advantages of modern society such as the university as restricted to white people. To express this exclusivist ontology, Kant deployed a racialized epistemology; and in order to explain this, Lu-Adler adopts David Theo Goldberg's description of racism as: a racially-based distribution of 'social power' whereby the dominant race is 'in a position to exclude [racial] others from (primary) social goods, including rights, to prevent their access, or participation, or expression, or simply to demean or diminish the other's self-respect (Lu-Adler 2022, 319). Applying this to Kant, Lu-Adler shows him to have portrayed the four races he identifies—white, yellow, black and red—in terms of unbridgeable differences. Whites, Kant asserts, possess all the driving forces, predispositions, and talents that are needed for advanced culture and civilization; they alone can continue to progress in perfecting themselves. Accordingly, it is primarily negative features that Kant attributes to his other three races.

The norm in academic circles, however, is to ignore, deny or downplay Kant's racism. For example, Kleingeld argues that Kant changed his mind and became less racist (Lu-Adler 2022). This argument, however, seems untenable since Kant maintained his moral indifference to the question of slavery, viewing its success as necessary for European prosperity and seeing the 'Negro' as a natural slave (Kant 2007; Lu-Adler 2022). The value of his model of moral universalism is undermined; yet many of his constructs remain valuable, and there is no reason to reject his whole philosophy; rather, like Habermas and others, one can be influenced by it but also seek to remedy it. Indeed, the university curriculum could be greatly enhanced by reading one Kant (the universalist) against the other (the racist) to see if the negligent lack of attention paid to Kant's taxonomy of race helps with understanding the as yet unresolved bias blind spot (Pronin, Lin, and Ross 2002).

As it stands, however, the negatives of difference from Kant are still very much alive on campus, and very poorly addressed—hence their perpetuation. Wael Hallaq (see Sect. 2.7) might have been classified as red-skinned by Kant and therefore deemed not capable of a conversation on the matter, yet Kant and Hallaq 'agree' on the need for independent universities; and here I argue for independent debate in universities.

3.3 Communities of Inquiry

I conduct debates on campus through *Communities of Inquiry*[1] (acronym CofI, pronounced *coffee*) sessions, which seek to provide agency through conversations that lead to action: it is an organising principle, not a method per se, and it opens a safe consensual space for challenging thinking and talking about doubts. A CofI group can be convened at any time and agree to discuss any topic. The topic may be pre-chosen as one that is of urgent interest or may be chosen by the group. The individuals may be staff, students or both. A session usually needs two hours to achieve a working rhythm of discussion and an outcome. Chatham House rules obtain i.e. what is said in the group stays within the group. Ideally a trained facilitator will support the group. University students who have learnt consent training, mediation and conflict resolution work are ideally placed to also train in CofI techniques and act as facilitators for CofI sessions. If that is not possible, then an individual will need to agree to intervene if there is abuse or severe upset: and in fact, each member should see themselves as a mediator of meaning for the benefit of group functionality (see Sect. 3.4). This is a development of the community of inquiry set out in *Pragmatism* by the pragmatist and scientist William James (1842–1910), who proposed its mediating role in group decision-making in general terms. This was quickly adopted by American pragmatist thinkers Charles Sanders Peirce (1839–1914) and John Dewey (1859–1952) who applied it to scientific problem-solving and democratic processes respectively. Peirce understood it as a way to move away from the Cartesian individual who worked out his own truth, towards the individual working in a group to share and evolve ideas in order to resolve doubts through inquiry:

> Doubt is an uneasy and dissatisfied state from which we struggle to free ourselves.... The irritation of doubt causes a struggle to attain a state of belief. I shall term this struggle Inquiry. (Peirce 1958, 99)

Peirce's contemporary, Nobel Peace Prize winner, friend to John Dewey and inspiration for the Chicago school of sociology Jane Addams, implemented it daily for twenty years in her work supporting immigrant women in the 19th District, Chicago. In fact, she likely understood Hull House—a multi-purpose safe house which functioned for 40 years, providing medical, educational, cultural and social community support, and which was the physical site of her activism—as a living example of a community of inquiry (Shields 1999); the women being supported there also conducted ground breaking social research and used their findings to bring about change in legislation (Shields 1999; Addams 1910, 126).

After these seminal thinkers, the community of inquiry was deployed with specific topics in mind. For example, Garrison used it to develop online communities (Garrison and Arbaugh 2007), Lipman and Kennedy to develop philosophical inquiry for children (Kennedy 2012), and Patricia Shields in her work on public administration (Shields 2003).

---

[1] I pluralise 'community'; 'CofI' is an acronym for my version.

The *Communities of Inquiry* approach preempts and precludes the prevalent dynamics of discourse explained by John Peters in 2005 (Peters 2005). He describes how, both on and offline the following sequence is now recurrent: in the name of liberalism an 'outrage artist' breaks a taboo with the use of a word or a sentiment that arouses support from a libertarian who wants to support free speech at all costs even when offence is caused. The third protagonist is the 'outraged bystander', the offended party who disagrees strongly, possibly for a range of different reasons (Peters 2005 cited in Titley 2020, 116–17). These three converge to co-create tension, heightened emotion and no resolution. *Communities of Inquiry* is very different, using, for example, the dubitative form of open questioning where doubt is shared openly: 'Why do you think that?' 'What do you mean?' What can we do about X?' This allows for doubt, for questioning and for negotiation. The optative form is also crucial: 'Let's hope for…,' 'May we succeed in ….,' 'Let there be…' (Ricœur 1965, 205–208). The optative form expresses possibility, future intention that can be dismissed as 'wishful thinking' that almost elides present and future tenses, so that the possible seems real. Optative language can in fact help us to hope for a better future by imagining it. Ricoeur looks at the optative in both religious and secular contexts and never underestimates the fallibility of hope (Ricœur 1994, 2001).

Communities of Inquiry emphasize that human understanding is fallible because individuals are materially affected by changeable factors such as social relations and context. In practice, it becomes a form of self-managed discussion in which participants can reflect on their beliefs and ask themselves and others whether they really have a clear understanding of an issue or whether they are in thrall to unverifiable opinions; and, if the latter, whether they wish to explore them critically or defend them unchallenged (Pardales and Girod 2006; Scott-Baumann 2010).

My development of *Communities of Inquiry* aligns with Jane Addams' solution-focused pragmatist philosophy in three ways: group identification of a problematic situation; a methodical, group-based approach to finding solutions by using different methods and approaches (as also recommended by Ricœur); and an emphasis upon participatory democracy, which necessitates having an open mind and listening to different viewpoints. These organising principles can provide a powerful antidote to the free speech wars that currently polarise debate into apparently simple binaries, and which make it seem as if we want either completely free speech or no free speech, unlimited immigration or no immigration, full access to rights or no access to rights, two sexes or no sexes etc.; in reality of course, decisions and practices are much more complex than 'all or nothing'.

3.4 Key Guidelines for Communities of Inquiry

To ensure proper discussion and debate, *Communities of Inquiry* last at least 90 min and can go on for several hours. There are five key guidelines that underpin *Communities of Inquiry*, which are listed below. They share many similarities with Habermas' ethics of discussion, who insists upon universal participatory and practical rules to govern any discussion and to resolve the tension between the individual, the group and society (Habermas 1984, 1987). Ricœur became interested in Habermas' communicative ethics late in life as a very different approach to that of either Kant or Rawls, with whose theory of justice he became somewhat disenchanted (see Sect. 6.3); Ricœur summarised Habermas' rationalist approach—which Ricœur had in fact practised for decades—as follows:

> Everyone has the right to speak; everyone has the duty to give his best argument to anyone who asks for it; he must be heard with a presumption that he could be correct and, finally, the antagonists of a rule-governed argument must share a common horizon which is one of agreement, of consensus. (Ricœur 2007, 240)

Ricœur continues:

> It assumes on the part of the antagonists an equal will to seek agreement, a desire to coordinate their plans of action on some reasonable basis, and finally a concern to make cooperation prevail over conflict in every situation of disagreement. (Ricœur 2007, 241)

I believe this is in fact a clear description of what can be achieved in a community of inquiry, but I do not find Habermas' three assumptions justifiable, or workable as 'rules', in the current fevered context of offensive language. I therefore propose that each group needs to establish their own rules in order to reach Habermas' three assumptions. I call this procedural ethics, which creates explicit ownership of agreed behaviour, takes account of cultural sensitivities and develops understanding of group identity as well as the incontrovertible individuality of each participant.

The absence of trust building in Habermas' model is noted by Danielle Allen, who posits that trust is vital so that one is not to be suspected of manipulation—a concern Plato also had (Habermas 1984, 1987; Allen 2004, 54–68). Ricœur too may have sensed the frailty in Habermas' insistence upon unanimity without building trust: he calls the model 'courageous' but notably confines his own discussion of it to legal and medical cases (where there are already sectoral frameworks within which to negotiate solutions); he avoids exploring more expansive moral debates in this context (Ricœur 2007, 241ff).

However, times have changed, and the culture wars have greatly distorted people's understanding of how to express themselves, with trust seemingly having completely disappeared. Furthermore, the culture wars have cemented extreme populist positions of left and right, with binaries so polarised that we cannot find agreement between two poles; the poles are contrived to be so far apart that they cancel the other out (e.g. leaving or remaining within the EU; deciding to support either sex or gender as the definitive identity marker). Hidden within such extremes are denial and negation because the process necessitates negating one pole of such an argument. This is not conducive for appreciating the nuances and complexities of the debates, nor for producing more amicable relationships. For that reason, I developed with Simon Perfect the fourfold discussion model explained in Chap. 1 (see Sect. 1.1), which Stephen Whitehead and Pat O'Connor have endorsed in *Creating a Totally Inclusive University* (Whitehead and O'Connor 2022). Using the model, interlocutors can determine the parameters of their discussion by choosing from libertarian, liberal, guarded liberal, or no-platforming models. Whilst libertarian and no-platforming are both extreme positions, each has a less headstrong sibling: the libertarian view is related to the liberal approach that we may speak openly as long as it is legal. The no-platforming approach is related to the guarded liberal view that we should take more care than usual with how we express ourselves, but that we should definitely discuss difficult issues. With all four options, there has to be clarity and agreement about the approach being adopted; additionally, with the extreme versions the discussion has to be especially carefully managed due to the risk of being trapped into extreme positions. Above all, knowing the options and being able to choose allows us to then act by discussing what to do instead of being intimidated or confused into silence by 'Populism's Pincer Grip' of extreme forms of libertarian or no-platforming reacting to each other (see Sect. 1.5).

Accordingly, the guidelines for *Communities of Inquiry* are as follows:

1. We need to take care with the words we use

Procedural ethics are necessary to ensure that individuals in a group are able to feel safe. To label this process as cancel culture negates its value; we have to be responsive to the linguistic toxicity obtaining in the world outside the university as a result of digital media, authoritarian populism and phenomena like the 'culture wars'. To avoid using confected accusations of insult that shut us down and stop us discussing urgent matters, as a society we need to relearn the etiquette of argument so that vocabulary can be used in discussion of controversial topics that seem negative. We must not forbid debate and discussion.

Ricœur offers us a clear method of thinking through this problematic with his exploration of the semiotic aspect of words and the related structural process that creates meaning—what he called 'a cumulative metaphorical process' (Ricœur 1974, 93). The word is capable of acquiring new layers of meaning while retaining the old ones; and a word can become a symbol that is a means of expressing an extra-linguistic reality which can be either useful or pernicious. A spoken word creates an event, located in time, space and sound that brings together the structure of language and the event created by our use of language. Each word potentially has many meanings, of which some may even contradict others (Ricœur 1974, 96): if we insist upon a single meaning, it will weaken our capacity to communicate.

Ricœur asserted that if we insist upon one particular meaning for a word, we close the universe of signs and thereby also close the possibility of discourse. In *Excitable speech* Judith Butler takes a similar view, believing that injurious words can be partially neutralized by being used and becoming a 'linguistic display that does not overcome their degrading meanings, but that reproduces them as public text and that, in being reproduced, displays them as reproducible and resignifiable terms' (Butler 1997, 100). However, the current atmosphere seems to me to militate against this approach. Some words have become so painful that they should not be used, even descriptively. Indeed, Butler goes on to explain why that might be the case, but also why it necessarily cannot remain so:

> No-one has ever worked through an injury without repeating it: its repetition is both the continuation of the trauma and that which marks a self-distance within the very structure of trauma, its constitutive possibility of being otherwise. There is no possibility of not repeating. The only question that remains is: How will that repetition occur, at what site, juridical or nonjuridical, and with what pain and promise? (Butler 1997, 102)

The *Communities of Inquiry* approach provides a site for refusal, replacement and review of terms, phrases or concepts that evoke discomfort or disgust.

2. It is unacceptable to refuse to discuss anything. The CofI group agrees upon the importance of discussing intractable problems as a principle, and then agrees on a topic to discuss together with a view to finding solutions.

Through group discussion, the topic of racism often emerges as being of interest. However, if, despite the group interest in discussing racism, one group member (perhaps in an influential position in the university with regard to race issues) says it is complicated to discuss race as a topic, the group may be tempted to drop the topic. But, more fruitfully, the question 'Why can we not talk about race?' could itself become the topic of discussion. Saying 'No' to a topic is discouraged. However, the 'invisibility' of whiteness, which confers privilege and power upon white members of the group, necessitates consideration of whether the group, if ethnically mixed, should meet a few times to get to know each other before having such a discussion. Safe spaces and expert advice could also be requested if required.

Bearing in mind Ricœur's conviction that the methods we choose and the questions we ask will determine where we end up, it is worth being pragmatic and initially choosing a topic in which the individuals believe there is a reasonable chance of deciding upon and agreeing upon a practical outcome.

3. The CofI group adheres to procedural ethics, which entail a commitment to the interests of securing group agreement.

Procedural ethics address the moral need to behave towards each other in ways that are reciprocal as well as agreeing to share the risk of causing offence and on the consequent need to apologise. (This is at odds with current use of social media.) Such a practical approach will help staff and students at universities to respond to the structural pressures currently driving the free speech wars on campus and to the systemic racism that endures.

Collective identity needs to be established by deciding upon the parameters of discourse (Scott-Baumann and Perfect 2021). Since this establishment of parameters may end up being a lengthy process, sufficient time needs to be set aside for it. It may even take up the bulk of the session; but, in the process, participants will be able to face and deal with the tensions in language that underpin their positions. Through this process, definitions of terms can be clarified, and participants may even agree that some language and some ideas will not be used in their CofI—but may be reserved for future discussions (see above).

4. Participants must see themselves as group members, willing participants in group change, where each participant is also a mediator between their

'truth' and that of the others: participants 'must be hospitable and ready for experiment' (Addams 1910, **126**).

Using evidence is often convincing, but there is so much 'fake news' available, that we need to make decisions about which sources we trust and whether we can secure information from different sources for comparisons. Participants join the CofI with the mindset that their 'truth' and arguments are there to be tested, and should have appropriate evidence to support their claims.

5. The group agrees to decide upon a practical goal, however small, that can be implemented after the discussion. Lobbying for change is practical if well planned.

For a community of inquiry to succeed, its members need to believe that they can take calculated risks together, towards a shared goal. Lobbying for change could range from asking to see the university's policies on a certain topic to working towards influencing a person of influence within the university, or beyond (an MP or peer, for example). Institutional needs may prevail: using *Communities of Inquiry* approaches I have been asked to teach deans and associate deans about 'whiteness' for example.

Addams was fearless in her belief that a small group can change laws: she lobbied successfully for many changes, including legal protection for children under fourteen from being used in factory labour. In all this activism she saw the need to find out what others wanted, learning from discussions in the onsite café at the Hull House:

> The experience of the coffee-house taught us not to hold preconceived ideas of what the neighborhood ought to have, but to keep ourselves in readiness to modify and adapt our understandings as we discovered those things which the neighborhood was ready to accept. (Addams 1910, 132)

I will show in Chap. 7 how *Communities of Inquiry* can contribute to what I call a 'politics of pedagogy', and how these organisational principles can be equally applied beyond the campus, including even the Houses of Parliament to become polity praxis (see Sects. 7.9 and 7.10).

3.5 Practical Outcomes

A key feature of *Communities of Inquiry* is for participants to consider concrete outcomes as a result of their dialogue. Whilst it is valuable to agree some possible outcomes at the initial stage, it is often the case that as the discussion evolves, different, sharper, and more pertinent goals will also emerge. They will be revisited and possibly renegotiated in the last fifteen minutes. In this plenary stage, and in the days that follow, participants will realise that they have negotiated a difficult conversation by using a moral framework that reminds them to be responsible for the words they use, and they can use the same processes in other discussions and debates. Furthermore, participants will also likely want to meet up again and return to the same group and topic to further the debate. As the group works on the concrete outcomes they collectively agreed, the opportunities for further discussion will also present themselves.

Such post-CofI steps heighten participants' appreciation of the value of collective discussions, and listening to understand different perspectives, rather than simply rebutting, refuting and rejecting. Through such steps and prolonged interpersonal engagement, individual members begin to appreciate that it is appropriate to subsume one's individuality just enough within the group that it becomes possible to retain one's own opinions (that may differ from the majority of the group) and contribute to a shared opinion that can drive an agenda forward productively to a useful practical outcome that may lead to working beyond the university, for example with parliament, in a form of polity praxis. By talking about issues in this way, participants start to see that it is more likely there will be worthwhile outcomes if people work to develop group understanding that encompasses individual views, even if partially. The personal sacrifice required when one is convinced of being 'right' becomes worthwhile for group cohesion, as I will show in the work of Danielle Allen (see Sect. 7.6) (Allen 2004).

3.6 Group Work

This description of group praxis is, however, also idealistic, and the concept of group cohesion is fragile. In a community of inquiry, the group becomes the context for decision-making, so it is necessary to consider the possible influence of the individuals who comprise it and the decision-making process. The process of doing so addresses the major challenge Ricœur presents us with: in order to balance different views, we have to recover the use of language that will allow us to create dialectical debate and explore the views of those we disagree with, instead of rejecting them. Hallaq explains that in the Islamic tradition, argument and debate (*ḥiwār*) were believed to be 'a primary precondition for knowledge and its acquisition' and that ideally the logical 'communicative dialectical methods formed, and were formed by, tradition' (Hallaq 2019, 52). Individuals and groups will use different means to influence each other, and a much-contested area is that of rhetoric: using form and emotional appeal to influence the decision making of others; the question often asked is whether this is acceptable or not.

3.7 Rhetoric: Plato's Gorgias Dialogue

In our university context, before we can be confident of conducting ethically valid group discussion, we must consider the suspicion of rhetoric as a beautiful yet deceptive use of language. Rhetoric is often perceived as a threat to effective group work. Plato, Socrates and Ricœur were deeply suspicious. Plato's Socratic Dialogues embody and exemplify a belief that discussion is the best and indeed morally the only

3.7 Rhetoric: Plato's Gorgias Dialogue

way to resolve differences. Its basis is Socrates' avowed assertion that ignorance is the basis for most human decisions, attitudes and beliefs, and that if we interrogate our own ignorance through honest discussion, we may find out what we don't know and, in the process, come closer to better understanding.

Arguing against oratory or oration (a form of rhetoric), Socrates used a form of dialectic based upon questioning in order to get the answers he wanted and suggested that: 'Oratory is a producer of conviction-persuasion and not of teaching-persuasion concerning what's just and unjust' (Plato 1987, sec. 455a). He attacked Gorgias and other rhetorician orators, objecting that to be a successful sophist it is not necessary to know your subject matter since it is like cookery or poetry; it is the art of persuasion, and thus about form rather than content; and that the act of oratory is always based upon flattery, persuasion, manipulation and power (Plato 1987, secs 466a-c, 464d, 481b, 466c–e).

Discussing Socrates' eponymous dialogue with Gorgias, and Plato's analysis of flattery as crucial to oratory, Ricœur describes oratory as 'the art of inducing persuasion by means other than the truth' (Ricœur 1965, 257). Ricœur sees the Gorgias dialogue as demonstrating the perversion of philosophy through sophistry and the perversion of politics through tyranny; he therefore summarises Gorgias in this way: 'Thus the lie, flattery and untruth—political evils par excellence—corrupt man's primordial state, which is word, discourse and reason' (Ricœur 1965, 257). A primordial state and reason resonate with Islamic *fiṭra*.[2] Resonant with Ricœur's hopefulness, Ovamir Anjum juxtaposes *fiṭra* with the deep scepticism about human nature and the world of Marx, Nietzsche, and Foucault (Hallaq and Anjum 2022, vol. 6).

In Plato's *Gorgias* dialogue, Callicles (pronounced Calliclees) remains proudly bullish about the use of language to get his own way, and his belief that the powerful are good: might is right[3]; so forceful arguments and elegant turns of phrase (clever, passionate and emotional but not always based upon evidence) are good. How do we balance the desire to persuade others of our way of thinking with the need to be honest and straightforward? In the Islamic tradition, *munāẓara* can serve to provide such balance and temper excess. It means 'examining mentally or investigating, by two parties, the relation between two things in order to evince the truth' and its etiquettes include the debating person being wary of extreme brevity; verbosity; using vague

---

[2] The Islamic theological concept of *fiṭra* (natural disposition) pertains to the 'active inclination of human beings towards recognition of God and worshipping him…'; furthermore, due to it, 'basic norms of morality are rationally knowable to a human actor in the state of *fiṭra*' – a state which plausibly includes 'both ontological and epistemological dimensions of morality (Harvey 2018, 14–15). Abdal Hakim Murad describes *fiṭra* as: 'the primordial natural disposition, which is related to the original Abrahamic religion, and therefore synonymous with the idea of authenticity; it is living in a way that is commensurate with what is natural for human beings - a natural style of life and inhabiting the fullness of our humanity' (Murad 2022, 18.30–22.00).

[3] Cf. Anjum on Islam being paradigmatically a religion of justice and thus fundamentally opposed to the might is right thesis; Anjum rues the tragic irony that a might is right 'theology of domination' has taken root in the Muslim world in the wake of European colonialism (Anjum 2022, sec. 1.45–5.30).

or unfamiliar words; interrupting before comprehending something; being offensive or vulgar (Taşköprüzāde 2020, 47, 52–54).[4]

In contrast to Socrates, through whom Plato voiced concerns about rhetoric, it was Aristotle, Plato's pupil, who admired, mastered and systematised rhetoric. In *Rhetoric*, he sets out the rules, giving both practical examples and theoretical structures that also explain why people are convinced by certain uses of language. Sam Leith argues that Aristotle understood that study of rhetoric was the study of human nature (Leith 2016, 3–31). In early medieval times Aristotle's work fell out of favour; however, with the accession of the Abbasids to power in Baghdad, and 'supported by the entire elite of Abbasid society', the Graeco-Arabic translation movement saw Islamicate scholars seeking out and translating such texts as Aristotle's *Rhetoric*, often saving them from destruction: indeed, 'from about the middle of the eighth century to the end of the tenth, almost *all* non-literary and non-historical secular Greek books that were available throughout the Eastern Byzantine Empire and the Near East were translated into Arabic' and thus saved for posterity (Gutas p.1).[5] Muslim scholars, however, understood rhetoric and oratory positively due to the foundational Arabic text: the Qur'an. The Qur'an uniquely employs *rhymed-prose* throughout and across themes, stories, responses and topics (legal and otherwise) to argue for the good life and what is just; it seeks to *both* teach and convince of its truth *with* rhetoric (Abdul-Raof 2006; Chowdhury 2013); it thus transcends Socrates' dissection of oratory and Aristotle's binary analysis that something is either something or it is not.

Thus, we need not uphold the Socratic understanding of truth and rhetoric being mutually exclusive; rather the focus needs to be on the obligations participants in a discussion have to each other which are important for building a culture of reciprocity in universities. This is consistent with Ricœur's belief that the authors of a speech action cannot present themselves as ethically neutral, because neutrality would be impossible:

> All speech acts… commit their speaker through a tacit pledge of sincerity by reason of which I actually mean what I say. Simple assertion involves this commitment: I believe that what I say is true and I offer my belief to others so that they too will share it. (Ricœur 1991a, 217)

---

[4] Please refer to the source for more etiquettes, and to the footnotes for elaboration on the moral purposes behind them.

[5] Gutas elaborates: 'What this means is that all of the following Greek writings [an extensive list follows], other than the exceptions [i.e. literary and non-secular] just noted, which have reached us from Hellenistic, Roman, and late antiquity times, and many more that have not survived in the original Greek, were subjected to the transformative magic of the translator's pen' (p. 1).

3.8 Communities of Inquiry Sample: Challenging Callicles

Aristotle proposed three powerful rhetorical techniques: *ethos* ('trust me'), *logos* ('believe me') and *pathos* ('follow me'). Is it possible to persuade others without using these techniques? Use the notes below to have a go at resolving a fundamental dilemma: should we use rhetoric or not?

In *Talking to Strangers*, Danielle Allen entitles a chapter 'Rhetoric: a good thing' and presents therein Aristotle's book *Rhetoric* as a magnificent approach. Not sharing any of the doubts that beset Socrates, Plato and Ricœur, she asserts that a speaker must 'be precise about which emotions are at stake in a particular conversation', generate trust by convincing all her audience, and use her fluency to demonstrate how she makes personal sacrifices and shows solidarity even with strangers (Allen 2004, 157). So, for Allen the rhetorical ability to persuade people is invaluable and does not lead to deceit because it must be based in honesty. For her, the ultimate prize is what she calls political friendship, and to achieve that she recommends rhetoric because it represents fluent and convincing communication which is vital for improving the world. Callicles is different.

Callicles accuses the others of, in effect, hypocrisy, asserting that he will speak truly while they dissemble: he doesn't care. He then states:

> I believe that the people who institute our laws are the weak and the many.... They're afraid of the more powerful among men, the ones who are capable of having a greater share, and so they say that getting more than one's share is 'shameful' and 'unjust'. (Plato 1987, sec. 483b)

In stark contrast with the orator and with the uncompromising Callicles, Socrates believed a philosopher should avoid the use of charm, flattery and seductive language and respond well to questions: 'alternately asking questions and answering them, and to put aside for another time this long style of speechmaking' (Plato 1987, sec. 499b). How can we overcome the 'brute force' of an argument like that of Callicles, using a community of inquiry? It is worthwhile believing that although Callicles will not change, those who witness the standoff will learn from Socrates' arguments. Using a *Communities of Inquiry* approach, read Plato's *Gorgias* and Allen's arguments in *Talking to strangers* and debate the pros and cons of rhetoric.

References

Abdul-Raof, Hussein. 2006. *Arabic Rhetoric: A Pragmatic Analysis*, 1st ed. London: Routledge.
Addams, Jane. 1910. *Twenty Years at Hull-House*. New York: Macmillan.
Allen, Danielle S. 2004. *Talking to Strangers: Anxieties of Citizenship since Brown v. Board of Education*. Chicago, Illinois: University of Chicago Press.
Anjum, Ovamir. 2022. Rebellion in Islam with Professor Ovamir Anjum Interview by Paul Williams. https://www.youtube.com/watch?v=d9M7MVf6UfI.
Butler, Judith. 1997. *Excitable Speech: A Politics of the Performative*. New York: Routledge.
Chowdhury, Safaruk Z. 2013. *Introducing Arabic Rhetoric: Course Book*, 2nd ed. London: CreateSpace Independent Publishing Platform.
Dabiri, Emma. 2021. *What White People Can Do Next*, 1st ed. UK: Penguin.
Garrison, D., and J.B. Arbaugh. 2007. Researching the Community of Inquiry Framework: Review, Issues, and Future Directions. *Internet and Higher Education—INTERNET HIGH EDUC* 10 (December): 157–172. https://doi.org/10.1016/j.iheduc.2007.04.001.
Habermas, Jürgen. 1984. *The Theory of Communicative Action: Reason and the Rationalization of Society*. Translated by Thomas McCarthy, vol. 1. 2 vols. Boston: Beacon Press. https://bac-lac.on.worldcat.org/oclc/299390340.
Habermas, Jürgen. 1987. *The Theory of Communicative Action: Lifeworld and System: A Critique of Functionalist Reason*. Translated by Thomas McCarthy, vol. 2. 2 vols. Boston: Beacon Press.
Hallaq, Wael B. 2019. *Reforming Modernity: Ethics and the New Human in the Philosophy of Abdurrahman Taha*. Columbia University Press.
Hallaq, Wael B., and Ovamir Anjum. 2022. *A Critique of Modernity: The State and its Forms of Knowledge*, vol. 6. 6 vols. Re-Orienting Orientalism, Reforming Modernity & Towards an Ethics of the New Human. American Islamic College. https://www.youtube.com/watch?v=5cJRO3C9u00&list=PLg_sc8wcf6k8maFgdDbKZy8QFU2Dsbxyn&index=2.
Harvey, Ramon. 2018. *The Qur'an and the Just Society*. Edinburgh: Edinburgh University Press Ltd.
Hillman, Nick. 2022. "You Can't Say That!" What Students Really Think of Free Speech on Campus. 35. HEPI Policy Note. Higher Education Policy Institute. https://www.hepi.ac.uk/wp-content/uploads/2022/06/You-cant-say-that-What-students-really-think-of-free-speech-on-campus.pdf.
Kant, Immanuel. 2007. Of the Different Races of Human Beings (1775). In *Anthropology, History, and Education*, edited by Holly Wilson and Günter Zöller, 82–97. The Cambridge Edition of the Works of Immanuel Kant. Cambridge: Cambridge University Press. https://doi.org/10.1017/CBO9780511791925.007.
Kennedy, David. 2012. Lipman, Dewey, and the Community of Philosophical Inquiry. *Education and Culture* 28 (2): 36–53.
Leith, Sam. 2016. *Words like Loaded Pistols: Rhetoric from Aristotle to Obama*. New York: Basic Books.

References

Lu-Adler, H. 2022. Kant and Slavery —Or Why He Never Became a Racial Egalitarian. *Critical Philosophy of Race* 10 (2).

Murad, Abdal Hakim. 2022. The Thinking Muslim—Is Modernity Destroying the Human Mind?—with Shaykh Abdal Hakim Murad Interview by Muhammad Jalal. Episode 70. https://podcasts.google.com/feed/aHR0cHM6Ly9hbmNob3IuZm0vcy9jNzM4MzgOL3BvZGNhc3QvcnNz/episode/YTAwNThjNTEtY2NjYy00ZTJkLWJjYzMtOTQwOGEyZDZmOTAz.

Pardales, Michael J., and Mark Girod. 2006. Community of Inquiry: Its Past and Present Future. *Educational Philosophy and Theory* 38 (3): 299–309. https://doi.org/10.1111/j.1469-5812.2006.00196.x.

Peirce, Charles Sanders. 1958. The Fixation of Belief. In *Charles Sanders Peirce: Selected Writings*. Ed. Philip Paul Wiener, 91–112. New York: Dover Publications.

Peters, John Durham. 2005. *Courting the Abyss: Free Speech and the Liberal Tradition*. Chicago: University of Chicago Press.

Plato. 1987. *Gorgias*. Translated by Donald J. Zeyl. Indianapolis: Hackett Pub. Co.

Pronin, Emily, Daniel Y. Lin, and Lee Ross. 2002. The Bias Blind Spot: Perceptions of Bias in Self Versus Others. *Personality and Social Psychology Bulletin* 28 (3): 369–381. https://doi.org/10.1177/0146167202286008.

Ricœur, Paul. 1965. *History and Truth: Translated with an Introduction by Charles A. Kelbley*. Translated by Charles A. Kelbey. 2nd ed. Evanston, IL: Northwestern University Press.

Ricœur, Paul. 1974. *The Conflict of Interpretations: Essays in Hermeneutics*. Translated by Don Ihde. Evanston: Northwestern University Press.

Ricœur, Paul. 1991a. *A Ricoeur Reader: Reflection and Imagination*. Edited by Mario J Valdés. New York: Harvester Wheatsheaf.

Ricœur, Paul. 1991b. *From Text to Action. Essays in Hermeneutics (II)*. Translated by Kathleen Blamey and John B. Thompson. London: The Athlone Press.

Ricœur, Paul. 1994. Le Bonheur Hors Lieu. In *Où est le bonheur?*, ed. R.-P. Droit, 327–341. Paris: Le Monde Editions.

Ricœur, Paul. 2001. L'optatif du bonheur. In *Demain L'Église*, ed. J. Duchesne and J. Ollier, 33–40. Paris: Flammaration.

Ricœur, Paul. 2007. *Reflections on the Just*. Translated by David Pellauer. Chicago, Illinois; London: University of Chicago Press.

Scott-Baumann, Alison. 2010. Ricoeur's Translation Model as a Mutual Labour of Understanding. *Theory, Culture & Society* 27 (5): 69–85. https://doi.org/10.1177/0263276410374630.

Scott-Baumann, Alison, and Simon Perfect. 2021. *Freedom of Speech in Universities Islam, Charities and Counter-Terrorism*. Islam in the World. London & New York: Routledge, Taylor & Francis Group.

Shields, Patricia M. 1999. *The Community of Inquiry: Insights for Public Administration from Jane Addams, John Dewey and Charles S. Peirce*. Texas: Texas State University. https://digital.library.txstate.edu/bitstream/handle/10877/3979/fulltext.pdf?sequence=1&isAllowed=y.

Shields, Patricia M. 2003. The Community of Inquiry: Classical Pragmatism and Public Administration. *Administration & Society* 35 (5): 510–538. https://doi.org/10.1177/0095399703256160.

Taşköprüzāde, Aḥmad Khalīl. 2020. *A Treatise on Disputation and Argument*. Translated by Safaruk Z. Chowdhury, 1st ed. London: Dar al-Nicosia.

Titley, Gavan. 2020. *Is Free Speech Racist?* 1st ed. Debating Race. Cambridge, UK ; Medford, MA: Polity.

Whitehead, Stephen, and Pat O'Connor. 2022. *Creating a Totally Inclusive University*. London: Routledge. https://doi.org/10.4324/9781003277651.

Open Access This chapter is licensed under the terms of the Creative Commons Attribution 4.0 International License (http://creativecommons.org/licenses/by/4.0/), which permits use, sharing, adaptation, distribution and reproduction in any medium or format, as long as you give appropriate credit to the original author(s) and the source, provide a link to the Creative Commons license and indicate if changes were made.

The images or other third party material in this chapter are included in the chapter's Creative Commons license, unless indicated otherwise in a credit line to the material. If material is not included in the chapter's Creative Commons license and your intended use is not permitted by statutory regulation or exceeds the permitted use, you will need to obtain permission directly from the copyright holder.

Chapter 4
Ricœur's Early Language, Activism and Algeria

Abstract This chapter on Algeria, and Chaps. 5 and 6 on Nanterre and Chicago respectively, present certain historical and conceptual aspects of Ricœur's activism on campus and outline his intellectual development. I will demonstrate the irrefutable connections between his ideas and his applied work. As a junior academic, Ricœur held utopian ideas about the university as a site for self-development and rich educational opportunities for all, as well as a locus for political activism. In this chapter, I consider the role of the university campus in Ricœur's early to mid-career struggles with abuses of power in the idealism that followed World War 2, reflected through his philosophy. As a relatively junior academic, his approach, based on polemical discussion with students, was successful from 1947 in opposing colonial France in Algeria.

Keywords Shari'a · Algeria · Colonialism · Structuralism · Existentialism · Negation

4.1 Colonialism's Legacy in the Muslim World

Ricœur was highly successful in his anticolonial work, using discussion and debate with students to further the cause, as well as publishing articles. By reviewing the history of this period in his life we see clearly his success in using discussion to effect change. In his essay *Universal Civilisation and National Cultures*, Ricœur commented on the worldwide hegemony of European culture underpinned by the imposition of the nation state's colonial administration and physical force:

> No one can say what will become of our civilisation when it has rarely met different civilisations by means other than domination and conquest. (Ricœur 1964, 277)

He was critical of Europeans' ability to dominate places far afield that consequently found their own culture and collective personality weakened and colonised by the West. He addressed this both academically and practically by showing how the colonised needed to reassert their own personalities in order to shake off the colonial personality imposed upon them:

> The fight against colonial powers and the struggles for liberation were, to be sure, only carried through by laying claim to a separate personality; for these struggles were not only incited by economic exploitation but more fundamentally by the substitution of personality that the colonial era had given rise to. (Ricœur 1964, 277)

This resonates with Wael Hallaq's description of the fatal weakening of Shari'a[1] by western culture imposed by a dominating personality type using physical powers. Like Ricœur, Hallaq is profoundly sceptical about the nation state (Hallaq 2013). Both advocate the community as a moral and viable grouping. Ricœur had much to say about the cruelty of colonialism where the nation state encourages the privileged self to oppress the less privileged self. The binary here is the person and the other, the coloniser and the colonised, both of whom are situated in specific places and times: in Ricœur's case, France and Algeria in the 1950s.

Taking colonial issues as the thematic case study for this chapter, I will show how Ricœur used existentialist and phenomenological methods (see Sect. 4.3) to challenge French colonialism in Algeria, by means, respectively, of affiliation with mass student protest and careful personal analysis of the abuse of power. His early work in particular, and his engagement with structuralism are also instructive.

In order to tentatively frame the generalized societal animosity towards Islam, I begin by juxtaposing colonialism with what it destroyed in Muslim cultures, which were often Shari'a-grounded community-rooted and community-driven societies. Shari'a, in contrast to colonial domination by administration and physical force, is based upon revelation, and therefore 'persistent[ly] attempts to locate itself in a particular moral cosmology'. In this ontology, the moral-legal cultures of non-Muslims were respected and upheld, and they had recourse to their own courts to settle their affairs. In such a world, contra European colonialism, the objective was not to 'render them subservient to colonial economic and commercial imperatives', so there was no need for the 'generally violent break-up of the native social and political systems [...] essential to relieving the colonies of their wealth'; rather, 'the Shari'a, by the constitution of its $fiqh$[2] (as well as by its actual socioeconomic history), neither promoted economic classes nor encouraged capitalistic or class dominance' (Hallaq 2009, Chap. 13). By contrast, European colonialists imported the nation state to colonised territories to systemically and systematically control 'both the social order and the national citizen [...by] engag[ing] in systemic surveillance, disciplining and punishment [and via] its educational and cultural institutions' thereby converting the Muslim believer into the good colonial servant who could be economically exploited

---

[1] Shari'a 'should be understood as revealed normative discourses that have defined Islamic orthodoxy throughout history' (Mian and Moosa 2012). In Hallaq's elaboration, 'the Sharīʿa consists of the hermeneutical, conceptual, theoretical, practical, educational, and institutional system that we have come to call Islamic law. It is a colossal project of building a moral-legal empire whose foundational and structural impulse is summed up in the ever-continuing attempt to discover God's moral will' (Hallaq 2013, 51).

[2] 'In the formative years of Islam, $fiqh$ meant a juro-ethical understanding of revealed norms. After the first two centuries of Islam, $fiqh$ referred to professionalized schools of juro-ethical traditions that are referred to in European literature as Islamic law, a term now accepted by modern Muslims' (Mian and Moosa 2012). A $faq\bar{\imath}h$ is an expert in juro-ethical understanding of revealed norms/ legal rulings (pl. $fuaqah\bar{a}$).

as much as possible (Hallaq 2009, Chap. 13). Yet today, the topic of Shari'a can conjure up extreme forms of punishment such as used by some Taliban groups, rather than Hallaq's practical and accommodating pre-nation state depiction.

Shari'a's historically actioned, community-rooted, anti-exploitative idealism offers a refreshing localism that many people would find attractive; as Hallaq explains:

> internal, indigenous considerations of the community as the central domain of the moral would be the ultimate basis on which an evincive theory of antiuniversalism might be constructed, a theory that advocates the uniqueness of world societies but that also must summon up the intellectual stamina needed to provide a persuasive antidote to the dominating liberal concept of universalism. (Hallaq 2013: 168)

Fresh scholarship can release us from such dichotomous arguments (antiuniversalism versus liberalism), as in Scharbrodt's work on Muhammad Abduh as a scholar at ease with ambiguity and complexity as well as with decisive legal rulings (Scharbrodt 2022). Thus we could learn from Shari'a to reverse various postcolonial trends visible now, such as the urgent need to support small scale local government and local networks rather than centralizing control and funds and then starving the localities of finances. On this positive note, Vinding considers the potential for Shari'a to engage directly with state analysis and be an immanent agent for change (in Scandinavia specifically). However, he also indicates the complexity of this endeavor since Shari'a is mis/understood in such polarized ways that its meaning first needs to be clarified (Vinding 2022). As one instance of this, Fadel reminds us that Hallaq's inversion of morality regards modernity as oppressive, not Shari'a, which creates a false binary and may even preclude healthy critique (Fadel 2011: 123). Indeed, as Moosa points out, Islamic legal traditions can under certain circumstances make it impossible to countenance changes occasioned by human circumstances in case the belief system could lose its identity (Moosa 2009: 164–65).

4.2 Young Ricœur and Colonial Influence

Ricoeur avoided the prefix 'post' as in (for example) 'postcolonial' when possible, believing that most belief systems retained their identity and their problems even when apparently displaced. He experienced this throughout his long life. Born in 1913 and departing the world in 2005, European empire building, destruction and collapse of empire were significant themes throughout Ricœur's life, which featured several pressure points: familial, faith related and both national and international. As a child, he was an orphan brought up by grandparents: he reported that he often misbehaved at school and that, when training for the army, he was considered 'unruly'. By marrying into a family with anarcho-syndicalist connections, he became aware of socialism as a possible antidote to growing fascist tendencies after the First World War. As a young secondary school teacher, he was militant, taking part in the socialist youth movement, attending marches and supporting the socialist Popular Front. It seems unsurprising then that Ricœur became active in seeking freedom from colonialism for Algeria, despite being best known as a theoretical philosopher.

There are religious, international and political reasons for his sensitivity to power imbalances. At home, he was a Protestant family member of a minority religion in Catholic-heritage France. Internationally, in Ricœur's childhood and young adulthood, the French colonial system was strong. For much of the Second World War he was held in a camp as a prisoner of war. After witnessing the collapse of Germany's imperial ambitions, during his long life, he also witnessed the decline of other European imperial powers, particularly that of the French in Algeria. The hitherto dominant idea that western culture and white people are the bearers of superior civilisation was also coming under question.

Yet, at the time of writing (2022–3), we see that this idea of white supremacy still enjoys much currency, and it is met with both increasing challenge (such as the Black Lives Matter movement) and resentful reassertion from powerful groups (via a 'culture war' encouraged by state-affiliated interests that seek to deny issues such as racism and the need to decolonise the curriculum). Colonial injustices were of great concern to Ricœur decades ago, and this distinguishes him from many of his illustrious French forebears, including the political scientist de Tocqueville (1805–1859), who paid no attention to the French colonization of Algeria that took place in his lifetime, and Durkheim (1858–1917), the architect of modern sociology, who showed no interest in the French empire. Similarly, in Germany, Weber saw empire as a necessary adjunct to the nation state, and Marx, although critical of slavery, was intent upon analysing the cruelty of capitalist labour in the west. Indeed, since its inception the very discipline of sociology has, Bhambra and Holmwood argue in *Colonialism and Modern Social Theory*, remained negligent, willfully blind or dishonest about empire, colonialism, racism and slavery (Bhambra and Holmwood 2021). By contrast, in 1961 Ricœur wrote perceptively against the false belief that European and North American culture is superior to that of other continents, and rejected the hegemonic cultural mediocrity exported by the West:

> Everywhere throughout the world one finds the same bad movie, the same slot machines, the same plastic or aluminium atrocities. (Ricœur 1964, 277)

Ricœur understood the failure of borders to be accurate markers of nations or languages, showing how the prime purpose of a state was impossible. He was highly critical of the nation-state: he saw the danger of the state and the nation becoming one unit, and understood how limiting the individual to national identity has the potential to nurture nationalistic and thence even xenophobic impulses. In Ricœur's words:

> There is no political distribution of borders which is adequate to the distribution of languages and cultures, so there is no political solution at the level of the nation-state. This is the real irritant of the 20th century, this dream of a perfect equation between nation and state. (Kearney 2004, 146)

Hallaq's argument for the state's impossibility is rooted in his concern for 'ecological sustainability, along with moral and communal prosperity' and his focus thus pertains to the unsustainability of modernity's physical and human destructiveness (Anjum 2013, 134; Hallaq 2013). Here Hallaq recommends a dialectical method of resolution, as Ricoeur often did also:

This initial but sustained process is therefore dialectical, moving back and forth between the constructive efforts of community building and a discursive negotiation with—and of—the modern state and its liberal values, in both East and West. As we will see, insisting on the second component of this dialectic is as essential as the steadfastness with which the first component—the raison d'être of the entire project—is pursued. (Hallaq 2013: 168)

4.3 Ricœur's Philosophical Toolkit

Ricœur used not only such dialectical methods, but all the intellectual tools at his disposal to deal with injustice. Let me begin by stating what some of these instruments are. Phenomenology can be described as the study of our ability to perceive the world around us, and use that insight to understand ourselves better. Existentialism took several action-based forms, including the socialism of Jean-Paul Sartre (d. 1980), for whom existentialism was an ideology-based attempt to carry out ideologically sound actions (Scott-Baumann 2022, 292–305). There was also a kind of existentialism in the positive approach to societal improvement and personal interdependence of Gabriel Marcel (d. 1973) with whom Ricœur agreed more than he did with Sartre. Existentialism came to seem highly subjective and was displaced in the 1950s by structuralism, a very successful attempt to replace the subject's viewpoint (yours and mine) and personal responsibility with structures and coded analysis of language. Ricœur found structuralism useful for analysing language, but limiting if applied as a system for understanding the world. Hermeneutics influenced him later with its transformative focus upon linguistic interpretation (see Chaps. 5 and 6). Another approach that was available but not used by Ricœur was Islam, which, according to Malise Ruthven, 'is above all the religion of justice' (1984, cited in Rosen 1999, 154). (I note this in my determination to bring the 'other', the Muslim, into this discussion in a Ricœurian way.) Ovamir Anjum juxtaposes this quintessential feature of justice against the current might-is-right 'theology of domination' that has taken root in the Muslim world in the wake of colonialism[3]; to compound the tragic irony, this 'theology', Anjum laments, is being promulgated in the service of secular 'statist extremism' (Anjum 2022, sec. 1.45–16.00).

As a young philosopher Ricœur was a phenomenologist, believing that it is necessary to focus on consciousness as the source of direct experience and, following Husserl, concentrated upon the way we see the world on the assumption that this will determine how we understand it, as long as we exclude unnecessary confusions. For Husserl this was an extension of the Cartesian tradition, amplifying Descartes' apparent faith in the human processes of cognition to develop rational thought. The result of such an explicitly subjective view and the belief that we make the world through our cognition, is that science too becomes subjective—its 'objectivity' is relinquished. However, we will only see clearly if we can decide how to 'bracket off' the distractions constantly present around us and focus on important matters. This follows a tradition established by Socrates: we must take our conscious experiences

---

[3] Anjum posits that some 'nominally free' post-colonial Muslim nation states are even more colonised now than the Muslim world was in nineteenth century colonial times.

seriously and focus intently upon all that we experience, in order to understand better and avoid coincidental reaction to chance events. During his captivity in World War 2, Ricœur explored this credo by translating Husserl's phenomenological *Ideas* into French, writing in tiny script in pencil in the margins of the German text.

4.4 Algeria and Empire

Algeria is prominent in my analysis of Ricœur's early philosophy because it shows his relevance to colonial and postcolonial studies and its relation to his views on the abuse of power. It also shows us how he was able to use discussion to develop students' ideas on truth and justice. Ricœur's significant role in influencing French public discourse vis-à-vis the French colonies, Vietnam and Algeria has mostly been ignored,[4] and much work remains to be done in the Ricœur archives to further clarify his anticolonial thought and better understand the persistent influence upon modern culture of colonialism with its abusive power (Ricœur 1965b; Scott-Baumann 2021; Wolff 2021). I also contrast his approach to decolonizing in the 1940s–1960s with his failure in the 1970s–1990s on the USA campus to recognise the consequences of slavery: colonization of the body and soul.

Ricœur achieved his decolonizing influence regarding Algeria by exercising his right to speak out with students on campus and beyond, to assert moral agency and to be accountable as a French citizen, a public intellectual and a left-wing Christian, writing articles as president of the *Mouvement du Christianisme Sociale*. In his arguments he made use of existentialism, phenomenology, structuralism and anthropology and conducted intellectual debates that bore directly upon public attitudes.

In 1947 Ricœur wrote a paper entitled *La question coloniale* (*The Colonial Question*), through which he challenged his government to attend to the injustices and cruelty of colonialism, including chronic abuse of power, endemic racism and use of torture. Consistent with his personalist approach that emphasized personal responsibility, he warned against the nation state as the solution:

> They [subjects of colonial rule] are right to do as we did, to be willing to be free before it is time; they are wrong, just as we were, to want to go through that useless detour of the nation-state. (Ricœur 2021, 18)

He posits that:

> The goal of colonization is to disappear by itself. We can never repeat that loudly enough. The time scale and the process according to which French sovereignty (fully and very often without qualification) will have to give way to the political freedom of peoples, is a subordinate technical issue that demands competence. But the most beautiful civilizing work is aimed at equipping ever-growing areas of humanity for freedom. (Ricœur 2021, 18)

---

[4] For example the authoritative 2008 Vansina bibliography of Ricœur's writings bears no subject entry for Algeria or colonialism (Vansina 2008).

Yet, his unequivocal decolonial criticism sits in tension with his apparent belief that the colonizers are also civilizers. This tension is further complicated by his insistence that racism is the scourge of all colonialism, and holding himself responsible for being part of that scourge: 'I don't know much about French oppression in the colonies and I dread that my error is, mainly, a sin of omission in not informing myself' (Ricœur 2021, 1947).

After the publication of Frantz Fanon's (d. 1961) masterpiece *Black Skin, White Masks* in 1952, however, Ricœur could of course have informed himself, but I do not know that he did. Nor did he visit colonised lands and he accepted that this put him at a disadvantage in comprehending colonialism (1947). A year after *Black Skin, White Masks* was published, in 1953 Fanon moved to Algeria. There he experienced the truth of his conviction that 'The white man is locked in his whiteness. The black man in his blackness' (Fanon 2008, ix–x). There he continued his work as a psychiatrist by developing modern psychiatric practices in ways that showed how mental illness is characteristic to those oppressed by colonization. In 1961, the year he died from leukemia, he wrote in *The Wretched of the Earth*: 'There is thus during this calm period of successful colonization a regular and important mental pathology which is the direct product of oppression' (Fanon 2001, 201, 1961). Ricœur too was influenced by modern psychiatric practices, but without Fanon's insights into mental illness resulting from colonialism.

All the while, Ricœur insisted upon the moral necessity for peace in territories that had been part of the French empire and were still integral to what was known as the French Union: Cambodia, Laos and Vietnam (Ricœur 1951). He condemned the Vietnam war (1955–75), and in 1955, he wrote about an anti-imperial impetus that he hoped would end the cold war and was still hopeful of decolonisation within the French Union (the French colonies) (Ricœur 1955). Necessarily, however, his greatest focus remained Algeria since, unlike French territories further afield, it was under direct colonial rule for 132 years.

French public opinion against the Algerian war hardened when information on French atrocities and their torture of Algerians became available in 1957; public pressure led to the fall of the French government in 1958 (the Fourth Republic), and De Gaulle came to power to lead the Fifth Republic. The vicious seven-year war (1954–1962) which ended with Algeria's independence still sparks strong resentment and antagonism amongst Algerians today—especially since France clearly retains very strong colonial-type links with Algeria.

4.5 Ricœur Versus Sartre: L'insoumission (Insubordination)

In 1960, many young Frenchmen, some of them recent university students, were being sent to fight in Algeria. On 05 September 1960, Jean-Paul Sartre, with supporters, published a letter in the national newspaper *Le Monde* calling on these soldiers to believe they had the right to insubordination since the war was unjust, and they should thus desert. Ricœur disagreed strongly, arguing that France was not a fascist state and thus did not merit desertion; second, that actions such as desertion should not be used to help the Algerians fight as the objective was to get France out of the war; and third that mass protest, not individual acts of rebellion, would bring negotiations closer (Dosse 2000, 304). Ricœur's strong response to Sartre, *L'insoumission* (*Insubordination*), was published in *Christianisme Sociale* (Ricœur 1960). Ricœur's argument reflects his determination that we should all be fully responsible for our language and behaviour, which, as I will show, contrasts with populist rhetoric and with the structuralist assertion that meaning is inherent in language structures, and not in the person who speaks and acts. However, further debate led to Ricœur also signing a statement that absolved deserters from guilt. This episode illustrates his measured, responsible reasoning; at the same time he was indeed instrumental in mass student protests against the war in Algeria.

In France and Algeria pressure was mounting with feverish debates on Algeria's future: in January 1961, 75% of the French population voted in a referendum for Algeria to be freed; yet in April 1961 a group of French generals executed a coup to ensure that Algeria would remain under full French colonial rule. Ricœur was incensed and overrode his own belief that political declarations should not take place on campus: at the Sorbonne University where he was teaching at the time, he announced that current events transgressed political trust, which made it imperative to develop an attitude of active resistance together (Dosse 2000, 308). Jean Baubérot, who was a student at that time, told François Dosse about Ricœur's balanced approach:

> The way in which Ricœur managed the situation without absolutizing politics influenced us, because we didn't want to claim to be Algerian resistance fighters and we also refused to demonize the kids returning home from active duty in Algeria, whom some people treated as if they were torturers. (Dosse 2000, 309)

The French Government had been concerned about Ricœur's influence upon public opinion and upon students for some years, given his work with the left-wing journal *Esprit* and his presidency of the *Mouvement du Christianisme Sociale*, where he made clear his aversion to the torture used by the French army in Algeria (Dosse 2000, 302–303). On 9 June 1961, at 06.00, while Ricœur was marking examination papers at home before breakfast, the police arrived, searched his house for arms or Algerian fighters, found neither, and then arrested him under suspicion of collaborating in activities against the French state (Dosse 2000, 267–268, 308–309). This action against Ricœur was evidence of state discrimination against those who supported the Arab cause in Algeria.

Vicious discrimination against Arabs themselves in France reached its nadir later that year: on 17 October 1961, thousands of Algerians working in Paris organised a peaceful demonstration against a curfew that had recently been imposed by the French police *only* upon Algerian Muslims: this led to the infamous Paris massacre. On that night, and during subsequent detentions and torture, a lethal mix of religion, class, poverty and ethnicity was used to justify state authorised murder of Algerian

Muslims in Paris. As many as two hundred Algerian Muslims may have died—beaten to death, shot or thrown into the Seine to drown. These events have never been properly documented or atoned for in any way by the French state; in the 2022 French presidential election contest in which Emmanuel Macron (once a research assistant to Ricœur) had to, for the second time, fight off a serious challenge from the far-right populist Marine Le Pen, French voices were raised in vain again to persuade Macron to apologise.

4.6 Methodological Dialectics and Hermeneutics

Ricœur's methods can help us to dismantle populist binaries such as those used by Marine Le Pen. This is because he worked on questions of method all his life and used dialectics in moderation, urging caution, unlike those who develop extreme populist binaries like 'woke' and 'antiwoke' currently:

> …the idea of a unique and exhaustive dialectical understanding of the social dynamic must be exposed as false; dialectics is a method and a working hypothesis; it is excellent when it is limited by other possible systems of interpretation …. And when it is not in power. (Ricœur 1965b, 190)

Indeed, the manipulative binaries of populism can be better understood by using Ricœur's dialectic: this shows the difference between extremes that can broaden an argument as with Ricœur, and extremes that can narrow an argument, as with the divisive language of populism that narrows our knowledge base.

Ricœur was fascinated by central issues of knowledge and language. He concluded that the method we choose and the questions we ask in order to solve a problem will determine the outcome. The position we start from will determine where we end up. Pure scientists and social scientists are keenly aware of this. Of course, it is occasionally possible to start inductively and develop fresh ideas, but this is very rare because we depend on existing topics and existing language. The tendency in social science and the humanities is to use words as the measurement of reality; and since our chosen words affect the content of our inquiry, we thus risk only finding what we seek, i.e. the one half of a binary we select (whilst rejecting the other half). As an example of how this habit distorts our thinking, Ricœur used a dialectical approach to analyse the two terms 'ideology' and 'utopia' (Ricœur 1976). Using Marx, he described the negative connotations of 'ideology' as concealment and distortion and cites Geertz to consider the rhetorical powers of ideology, that seek to legitimate authority with words that distort reality. For utopia, using Thomas More's creation of 'nowhere' as an impossible ideal brings the possibilities of improving society, using many and usually contradictory and unrealistic predictions. Utopia subverts, whereas ideology adverts to authority. They seem inverse, yet they are similar: both ideology and utopia are delusional since they both arise from systemic distortions in our cultural imaginations; he shows their differences and similarities and their dialectical interconnectedness:

> We have to call upon the 'healthy' function of ideology to cure the madness of utopia and ... the critique of ideology can only be carried out by a conscience capable of regarding itself from the point of view of 'nowhere'. (Ricœur 1976, 28)

We can use this approach when angered by extreme populist assertions. To help us live with these uncertainties and confusions stitched into our lives, Ricœur also developed hermeneutic approaches: he interpreted reality through linguistic devices such as narrative. Stories open us to risk and create conflicting interpretations that involve self-understanding; this leads in turn to the tension that is necessary for possible improvement of some sense of self.

Ricœur adopted the phenomenological dependence upon the self as interpreter of reality and, in order to avoid the risk of narcissistic absorption latent in some phenomenology, invited the self to see itself reflected in the other: this is the other person who is ultimately incomprehensible yet bears similarities to the way we see ourselves. Through this antinomy, this insoluble tension between similar yet incompatible phenomena, we may be able to see ourselves afresh. In hermeneutics, the other is also represented in the tension created by the confusion of being faced with the multiple meanings of language.

History and Truth (Ricœur 1965b) is a collection of essays that shows clearly this tension between the methods we choose for exploring an object of interest, and our reasons for using the chosen methods: in *Negativity and Primary Affirmation*, an essay written at the height of the Algerian crisis, Ricœur chose a phenomenological method that also has a Kantian note of overcoming negativity by accepting our limits (Ricœur 1965c).[5] Kant's racism, to which I have drawn attention, cannot be ignored (as it often is; see Sect. 3.2), but his very important rationalist philosophy of limits that shows us the inadequacy of much of our understanding, can be argued to form the backbone of modern western philosophy. By reflecting, questioning and becoming aware of the limits of our knowledge, Ricœur believed we will be able to act morally; for Ricœur, as for Hallaq, there must never be a separation between methods and ethics, which is a theme he explored continuously. Ricœur wished for the ensuing benefits which are hard to achieve but potentially powerful, as long as we use language ethically:

> An 'open society', to use Popper's term, is one which acknowledges that political debate is infinitely open and thus prepared to take the critical step back in order to continually interrogate and reconstitute the conditions of an authentic language. (Kearney 2004, 137–38)

---

[5] The essay 'Negativity and Primary Affirmation' (1956) is Ricœur's only published work on negation. It is at the end of the second edition of *History and Truth* and was not published in English until 1965; *Négativité et Affirmation Originaire* (*Negativity and Primary Affirmation*) first appeared in *Aspects de la dialectique*, *Recherches de philosophie*, II, Desclée de Brouwer, 1956, pp.101—124.

4.7 Linguistic Analysis and Structuralism as Method

'Consciousness is not a given but a task' and language is the instrument that provides both the methodology for better understanding of the self and others and also the content of such thought (Ricœur 1974b). In his journey towards these conclusions, Ricœur taught university courses on ancient philosophy and modern thought, including structuralism, and wrote detailed notes in preparation for them all. Many of these lectures inspired a Ricœur paper, a book chapter, a book or all three.

For structuralists, linguistic laws can be applied to language in order to know which linguistic codes operate and how binary oppositions can be used to identify and predict language patterns. Lévi-Strauss developed Saussure's analysis of linguistic binaries into a system that he believed would provide a taxonomy of societies. Ricœur could see the utility of applying these principles as a linguistic science for understanding language structures and possibly even for mapping pre-identified life patterns such as kinship or incest in supposedly less sophisticated cultures. He made use of structuralism for linguistic analysis, but rejected completely the use of its cool, systematic analysis that seeks deeper textual meaning and avoids implicating the human when looking at cultural aspects that cannot be defined in advance (Ricœur 1974a); for culture-cum-philosophy he preferred something more Hegelian that focuses upon meaning with 'a logic which would be that of contents not of syntaxes' (Ricœur 1974a, 51).

His 1960 publication *Symbolism of Evil* thus explores the phenomenological ways in which we actively interpret objects, words and ideas as symbolic—as representing something else (Ricœur 1967). With regards to 'sin', in *Fallible Man*, he recounts how three images recur repeatedly in Christian religious narrative: the fall, the stain, and the deviation from the path; and he warns against too zealous a condemnation of oneself, as that could lead to belief in original sin and possibly a debilitating lack of self-belief and lack of agency (Ricœur 1965a). In Islam, there is no concept of original sin since Adam and Eve inhabiting the earth was preordained for humans to take on the role of trustees, and there is no 'stain' associated since God taught Adam the words of repentance to compensate for the 'slip' (Harvey 2018, 14). Neither interpretation would be viable in structuralist thought, which would focus upon meaning as carried by syntax more than by semantics as carried by the reader. And yet Ricœur did not reject structuralism—as many did; rather, in order to get to grips with it, he brought together the philosophers of the journal, *Esprit*, and they met as a group for a year to discuss *The Savage Mind*, Lévi-Strauss's 1962 structuralist masterpiece. This exemplifies Ricœur's determination to climb inside a structure of thought and master it in order to understand and deploy both its limitations and its utility (Dosse 2000, 349).

4.8 Activism Beyond Negation

In the 1950s, Ricœur published his first major book *Freedom and Nature* (1950/1966 English), which was followed by *History and Truth* (1955/1965), *Fallible Man* (1960/1965) and *Symbolism of Evil* (1960/1967). In this sequence of works he grappled with human fallibility, frailty and the capacity to do wrong. It was also in the early 1950s that he started lecturing on negation, i.e. the ways we reject that which we don't like and also measure ourselves by lack, longing and loss rather than by what we have and who we are; and for twenty years he deliberated upon the concept, hoping to develop a philosophy of negation that would provide a both/ and model of addressing problems, to replace the binary either/ or (Scott-Baumann 2013, 129). His students at Strasbourg, the Sorbonne, Nanterre and, to a much lesser extent, Chicago experienced the material arranged in different sequences depending on who he imagined negation to have arisen from: among others, the ancient Greeks, Plotinus and Sartre, each in different ways. The students were his witnesses and he explained to them in his lectures how he was developing the theme of negation with them from one term to the next (Ricœur, n.d.). By the time he abandoned negation as a project in the 1970s, he had integrated the concept into his analysis of language: it became his deep and abiding conviction that the negative plays an integral part in our thought and our syntax, as is the case with metaphor; yet he saw how we seek to avoid, deny and reject the negative itself. If we are to make a better world, we have to accept that the negative resides in us all, and we cannot therefore simply use it as a way of distancing ourselves from that which we do not like.

Ricœur did not apply the negative impulse to decolonization: it was clear to him that colonial issues could not be solved by negative Sartrean existentialism, which measured worth by disruptive and ideologically driven activism, as happened in the *L'insoumission* (*Insubordination*) episode (see Sect. 4.5). Nor, with its focus on improving human perception, could phenomenology alone tackle the horrors of colonization since many, like Ricœur, did not visit and experience the colonies. So, instead, he combined phenomenological understanding of the self as an ethical being who is responsible for self-management but not entitled to command and control others—which he felt Sartre was attempting with the desertion proposal. Ricœur protested with students, wrote passionately in journals, used his left-wing Christianity as both structure and allegiance, and engaged directly with the philosophical movements that he found inadequate to the task. He enacted this as an academic and public intellectual, albeit sometimes naively, as we will see in Chap. 5.

4.9 Communities of Inquiry Sample: Discussing Decolonisation

Use the passage below and *Rethinking Political Thinkers* (Ramgotra and Choat 2023) to develop a working definition of decolonisation.

'Decolonising the curriculum' refers to the idea that the curriculum reflects western accounts of history and does so from a white, establishment perspective (conjuring terms such as 'dead white men'/'pale, stale and male'....) (Morreira et al. 2021). In order for history to be as full a record as possible, however, it would need to also tell others' stories by embedding the voices of minorities, those of colour and those who were dominated and exploited by the Belgian, British, French and Spanish empires. In Britain, decolonizing the curriculum becomes a matter of recognition for Africa. In *Africa is not a country: breaking sterotypes of modern Africa*, Dipo Faloyin describes how, following direct colonisation, from 1881 to 1914 seven European nations arbitrarily carved the African continent of over 6 million people speaking well over 1,000 languages into 54 territories; they became today's troubled nation states, many of which are still in thrall to European powers (Faloyin 2022); thus the cry for decolonisation and freedom from neocolonial realities remains strong and persistent.

A decolonized canon would not only clarify Britain's full history but also fully recognize the contributions of its peoples of colour. However, designing and implementing decolonized curricula would require a major shift in thinking from many educators and students, especially since it is hotly contested by many commentators, educators and politicians who want to preserve the traditions that present the British empire as a greater good (Olusoga 2016). To exacerbate matters, the government has incorporated it into the culture wars, accusing the university sector of making unreasonable and unjustifiable complaints.

Yet within this debate there are tensions too: when Britain focuses upon Africa as a target for decolonisation this can function as another form of colonization by applying a deficit model to a continent as if it is one country. In terms of what African nations themselves should be doing, one view is that of academics such as Olúf́ẹmi Táíwò who reject the 'decolonisation industry', arguing it is 'intellectually unsound', 'wholly unrealistic' and that it 'attacks its own cause'[6]; rather, Táíwò insists on a more positive view to find ways forward, arguing that the cultural hybridity that charactizes modern Africa can provide the continent with the strength to free itself—in its own way—from the decolonisation narrative (Táíwò 2022).

From a global perspective, in whichever way decolonisation can/ cannot be helpful, what is clear is that the economic and environmental crises cannot be tackled without tackling racism, class, slavery and its residues, and combatting the colonialism that is an integral part of all our systems of thought and the social structures of poverty and wealth (Craig 2022). Appreciating Kant's philosophical legacy yet challenging his racism would be productive, for example. Indeed Campbell argues that it's necessary to face pedagogical racism *in order to* decolonise the curriculum (Campbell et al. 2022).

References

Anjum, Ovamir. 2013. Hallaq's Challenge: Can the Shari'ah Save Us from Modernity? *American Journal of Islamic Social Sciences* 30 (3): 124.
Anjum, Ovamir. 2022. Rebellion in Islam with Professor Ovamir Anjum Interview by Paul Williams. https://www.youtube.com/watch?v=d9M7MVf6UfI.
Bhambra, Gurminder K., and John Holmwood. 2021. *Colonialism and Modern Social Theory*. Oxford: Polity Press.
Campbell, P., Ajour Ashjan, Andrew Dunn, Heena Karavadra, Keith Nockels, and Sarah Whittaker. 2022. *Evaluating the Racially Inclusive Curricula Toolkit in HE': Empirically Measuring the Efficacy and Impact of Making Curriculum-content Racially Inclusive on the Educative Experiences of Students of Colour in the UK*. Leicester: University of Leicester. https://doi.org/10.25392/leicester.data.21724658.v1.
Craig, Mya-Rose. 2022. 'Why We Can't Tackle the Environmental Emergency without Tackling Racism'. NGO. *Greenpeace UK* (blog). 21 July 2022. https://www.greenpeace.org.uk/news/environmental-racism-report-summary/.
Dosse, François. 2000. *Paul Ricoeur: Les sens d'une vie*. Paris: La Découverte.
Fadel, Mohammad. 2011. A Tragedy of Politics or an Apolitical Tragedy? *Journal of the American Oriental Society* 131 (1): 109–127.

---

[6] https://www.hurstpublishers.com/book/against-decolonisation/#:~:text=Ol%C3%BAf%E1%BA%B9%CC%81mi%20T%C3%A1%C3%ADw%C3%B2%20fiercely%20rejects%20the,scholarship%20on%20and%20in%20Africa.

References

Faloyin, Dipo. 2022. *Africa Is Not A Country: Breaking Stereotypes of Modern Africa*. London: Harvill Secker.
Fanon, Frantz. 1952. *Peau Noire Masques Blancs*. Collections 'Esprit'. Paris: Ed. du Seuil. http://catalogue.bnf.fr/ark:/12148/cb32091544r.
Fanon, Frantz. 1961. *Les Damnés de la Terre*. Cahiers libres. Paris: François Maspero, 40 rue Saint-Séverin, Ve.
Fanon, Frantz. 2001. *The Wretched of the Earth*. Translated by Constance Farrington. Penguin Modern Classics. London: Penguin Books.
Fanon, Frantz. 2008. *Black Skin, White Masks*. Get Political. London: Pluto. http://www.dawsonera.com/depp/reader/protected/external/AbstractView/S9781849644532.
Hallaq, Wael B. 2009. *Sharī'a: Theory, Practice, Transformations*. Cambridge, UK; New York: Cambridge University Press.
Hallaq, Wael B. 2013. *The Impossible State: Islam, Politics, and Modernity's Moral Predicament*. New York: Columbia University Press.
Harvey, Ramon. 2018. *The Qur'an and the Just Society*. Edinburgh: Edinburgh University Press Ltd.
Kearney, Richard. 2004. *On Paul Ricoeur: The Owl of Minerva*. Aldershot Hants: Ashgate.
Mian, Ali Altaf, and Ebrahim Moosa. 2012. 'Islam'. In *Encyclopedia of Applied Ethics. [Eds.] Ruth Chadwick, Dan Callahan and Peter Singer*, 2nd ed., 769–76. Elsevier. https://www.academia.edu/1641124/_Islam_Encyclopedia_of_Applied_Ethics.
Morreira, Shannon, Kathy Luckett, Siseko H Kumalo, and Manjeet Ramgotra. 2021. *Decolonising Curricula and Pedagogy in Higher Education: Bringing Decolonial Theory into Contact with Teaching Practice*. 1st ed. Thirdworlds. London: Routledge.
Moosa, Ebrahim. 2009. 'Colonialism and Islamic Law'. In *Islam and Modernity: Key Issues and Debates*, ed. Muhammad Khalid Masud, Armando Salvatore and Martin Van Bruinessen. Edinburgh: Edinburgh University Press.
Olusoga, David. 2016. Wake up, Britain. Should the Empire Really Be a Source of Pride? *The Guardian*, 23 January 2016, sec. Opinion. https://www.theguardian.com/commentisfree/2016/jan/23/britain-empire-pride-poll.
Ramgotra, Manjeet, and Simon Choat, eds. 2023. *Rethinking Political Thinkers*. New York: OUP Oxford.
Ricœur, Paul. 1947. La Question Coloniale. *Réforme* 3 (131): 2.
Ricœur, Paul. 1951. Pour La Coexistence Pacifique Des Civilisations. *Esprit* 177 (3): 408–419.
Ricœur, Paul. 1955. Vraie et fausse paix. *Autres Temps* 76 (1): 51–65. https://doi.org/10.3406/chris.2003.2409.
Ricœur, Paul. 1960. L'insoumission. *Christianisme Sociale* 7–9 (November). https://olivierabel.fr/ricoeur/ricoeur-l-insoumission.php.
Ricœur, Paul. 1964. Universal Civilisation and National Cultures. In *Histoire et vérité*. Paris: Seuil.
Ricœur, Paul. 1965a. *Fallible Man: Philosophy of the Will*. Chicago: Henry Regnery Co.
Ricœur, Paul. 1965b. *History and Truth: Translated with an Introduction by Charles A. Kelbley*. Translated by Charles A. Kelbey. 2nd ed. Evanston, IL: Northwestern University Press.
Ricœur, Paul. 1965c. Negativity and Primary Affirmation. In *History and Truth: Translated with an Introduction by Charles A. Kelbley*, 2nd ed., 305–28. Evanston, IL: Northwestern University Press.
Ricœur, Paul. 1967. *The Symbolism of Evil*. Translated by Emerson Buchanan. Boston: Beacon Press.
Ricœur, Paul. 1974a. Structure and Hermeneutics. In *The Conflict of Interpretations: Essays in Hermeneutics*, translated by Don Ihde, 27–61. Evanston: Northwestern University Press.
Ricœur, Paul. 1974b. *The Conflict of Interpretations: Essays in Hermeneutics*. Translated by Don Ihde. Evanston: Northwestern University Press.
Ricœur, Paul. 1976. Ideology and Utopia as Cultural Imagination. *Philosophic Exchange* 7 (1): 17–28.

Ricœur, Paul. 2021. La question coloniale. *Études Ricoeuriennes / Ricoeur Studies* 12 (1): 16–20. https://doi.org/10.5195/errs.2021.550.

Ricœur, Paul. n.d. «La Négation» Cours (c.1952–1970). Fonds Ricœeur, Paris. Ricoeur Archives AR/FR, BIB.IPT: Inv 1, dossier 96.

Rosen, Lawrence. 1999. *The Justice of Islam: Comparative Perspectives on Islamic Law and Society*. Oxford Socio-Legal Studies. New York: Oxford University Press.

Scharbrodt, O. 2022. *Muhammad 'Abduh: Modern Islam and the Culture of Ambiguity*. London: Bloomsbury.

Scott-Baumann, Alison. 2013. *Ricœur and the Negation of Happiness*. London: Bloomsbury.

Scott-Baumann, Alison. 2021. Ricœur and the Hermeneutics of Decolonisation on Campus. In *Renewing Hermeneutics: Thinking with Paul Ricœur*. Eds. Johann Michel and Carla Canullo, 273–90. Roma: InSchibboleth.

Scott-Baumann, Alison. 2022. Murdoch and Sartre. In *The Murdochian Mind*. Eds. Silvia Caprioglio Panizza and Mark Hopwood, 1st ed. Routledge Philosophical Minds. Routledge.

Táíwò, Olúf´ẹmi. 2022.*Against Decolonisation: Taking African Agency Seriously*. London: Hurst.

Vansina, Frans D. 2008. *Paul Ricœur, Primary and Secondary Bibliography: 1935–2008*. Leuven: Peeters.

Vinding, NV. 2022. Sharia and the Scandinavian Welfare States. *Scandinavian Journal of Islamic Studies* 16 (2): 8–20. https://doi.org/10.7146/tifo.v16i2.134801.

Wolff, Ernst. 2021. *Lire Ricœur Depuis La Périphérie*. Editions de l'Université de Bruxelles. https://library.oapen.org/handle/20.500.12657/48482.

Open Access This chapter is licensed under the terms of the Creative Commons Attribution 4.0 International License (http://creativecommons.org/licenses/by/4.0/), which permits use, sharing, adaptation, distribution and reproduction in any medium or format, as long as you give appropriate credit to the original author(s) and the source, provide a link to the Creative Commons license and indicate if changes were made.

The images or other third party material in this chapter are included in the chapter's Creative Commons license, unless indicated otherwise in a credit line to the material. If material is not included in the chapter's Creative Commons license and your intended use is not permitted by statutory regulation or exceeds the permitted use, you will need to obtain permission directly from the copyright holder.

Chapter 5
1968 and Campus Shock at Nanterre

Abstract This chapter explores the failure of Ricœur and Nanterre students to engage with each other through discussion. In the mid-1960s, Ricœur had sought an alternative higher education model to break the hegemony of the Sorbonne as a place of huge lectures, distant tutors and a classical education. He was sympathetic to the students' rebelliousness, yet his dream of equality of class, gender and subject discipline on campus failed; his experiences give us insight into the fragility of discussion as a mediating process.

Keywords Nanterre · 1968 · Freud · Populism · Gender · Hermeneutics of suspicion · Phenomenology

5.1 What Happened in 1968?

In the late 1960s Ricœur, now an important leading intellectual, was involved in setting up a new university for the Sorbonne at Nanterre. Nanterre University was an ambitious and innovative experiment intended to fulfil his dream of the open, egalitarian campus. This was hijacked by student unrest and led to him resigning as Dean of the Faculty of Letters after two years (1969–71). Here I show what happened to illustrate how his theories (analysed in Chap. 4) compare with events. My exploration of his 1968 experience will set clear historical boundaries between then and now, so we can see how much or how little progress has been made on campus.

In the 1960s Ricœur had a very good reputation among his students as a lecturer, and there are thousands of pages of detailed lecture notes held at the Fonds Ricœur archives that show how well he prepared each lecture and each sequence of lectures. But he was tired of the large impersonal lecture setup at the Sorbonne and wanted to break the sterile hegemony of this hierarchical model of higher education: he sought an alternative. This challenge led him to the mud pits of the building site for the new university, Nanterre, which was then a sprawling working-class suburb of Paris, where decrepit shantytowns housed Algerian migrant workers. Through his appointment there, Ricœur, in an idealistic leap of faith, wanted to broaden Paris's student population by attempting to overturn class and ethnic differences. This experiment ended badly for him, with police being called onto campus; this created disappointment and humiliation and exposed a deep gulf between his ideas and his practice. Consequently, his methods for facilitating change became less clearly phenomenological and existential (of the Gabriel Marcel mode) and more hermeneutic: from his aversion to colonial abuses, he carried over his determination not to use language as a form of conquest and domination to win an argument (see Chap. 4).

The débacle at Nanterre provides an instructive contrast with English universities both then and now, and highlights the question of what a university should be. In the 1950s and 1960s, French students, mostly white, middle class and male, particularly in urban conurbations, became suspicious of university management of the curriculum: they felt they were not being allowed to determine what they studied, and they were angry about world events involving France (Algeria) and America (the Vietnam war). Ricœur campaigned actively with students to end both wars. In the mid-1960s he saw more trouble brewing as students became increasingly discontented. The political iconography was potent: there were posters of Mao Zedong, who was uncritically admired as transforming China. Che Guevara and Fidel Castro (in Cuba) and Ho Chi Minh (in Vietnam) were admired for standing up to the USA. At the same time, Ricœur was working on the hermeneutics of suspicion and on negativity and was sensitive to the negativity of students' demands, agreeing with them that there was a lot at stake.

Contrarily, Vinen doubts whether much actually happened in 1968, suggesting that the French revolt of 1968–71 was focused upon a desire for better education and more rights and was therefore really just a manifestation of the individualism encouraged by increasing consumerism and other societal factors (Vinen 2018). Moreover, English university campuses from the1960s to the 2020s have rarely shown signs of rebellion, revolt or revolution. The posters which accompanied student protests in France were admired in the UK more as art than as symbols of liberation from tyranny.

I thus wonder what (if anything) political activism means to most English students; I wonder whether long-standing passivity creates a sort of crisis on campus which, in effect, now demands that we accept being ventriloquised by social media and being complicit with the powerful who govern our consumerised lives (Scott-Baumann 2019). Dispiritingly, Ricœur's activism may not have produced anything more fruitful, with his dream of better university conversations with students than those offered by the Sorbonne seemingly ending in the wastepaper basket which a Nanterre student rammed over Ricœur's head in exasperation.

Nevertheless, what happened in Nanterre is important for our understanding of Ricœur's philosophy and for delineating the limits and strengths of conversation as mediation, in which he placed so much trust. Given the festering twenty-first century crisis about free speech and academic freedom, this comparative analysis will also contribute to our understanding of university campuses now and for charting a way forward. The existence of women on campus and in philosophy was also becoming historically significant in 1968; yet, despite his general compassion and support for women staff and students (as commented upon to me by his friend Mireille Delbraccio in 2010), Ricœur's default position was male and white, which will become increasingly significant as the narrative evolves.

5.2 Ricœur's Commentaries on the University Crisis: 1968 and Beyond

The four Ricœur papers I outlined in Chap. 2 show us the progression, evolution and frustrations that motivated his thinking about university education and will form the framework for this chapter (Ricœur 1964, 1968a, b, 1971b). Further analysis of them here will show what has changed in the fifty-plus years since, and how much has stayed the same. By contrasting the 1960s with current developments, the twenty-first century English university can be shown to be symptomatic of a state that has been deliberately shrunken by successive governments with decreased interest in state-funded education and development of ideas.

The 1964 paper, *Faire l'Université* (*Making the University*), is the summary of an inquiry that he organised to look at how the university sector could manage the challenges facing it; it preceded by four years the staggering events of May 1968 which saw French students and unions working together to disrupt French society, and which even led President De Gaulle to flee the country briefly. Ricœur's student interviewees requested root and branch reform of what they experienced as the long drawn out, slow, dry pedagogic grind of huge lectures, seminars, workgroups and discussions—and one student predicted that without better organised teaching, staff would soon see their teaching called into question and students would see themselves as 'violated and infantilised' (Ricœur 1964). Ricœur supported these demands and also recommended that each student should have a folder kept on their academic and personal development, to offer maximal support and guidance (Ricœur 1964). No action was taken on his report, which probably had no formal authority, and so he continued to develop the idea of establishing a new university, animated by an approach that insisted upon listening to those with no authority or status; in this way, he paralleled the decolonizing ethos. His philosophy was egalitarian: he insisted that philosophy was only one form of knowledge, and never the ultimate arbiter.

Two remarkable elements stand out here in contrast to the campus today. First, in the 1960s Ricœur was very unusual in using this pedagogy that shares characteristics with decolonizing approaches which reduce the power differential between student and teacher. Believing that personal communication is crucial, he disliked intensely the huge Sorbonne lectures and being inaccessible as lecturer and craved the opportunity to discuss ideas with individuals and small groups of students. He implemented this by using informal interview methods to collect opinions from students. This approach is relatively common today; yet many students of colour still feel as if they are trapped in a colonial time warp (Scott-Baumann et al. 2020). Second, looking back on this vision, Ricœur's unquestioning confidence that the state would continue to view higher education as an enterprise to be supported and valued seems remarkable; by contrast, in England and Wales students are now customers who show their approval or otherwise of services rendered by means of student satisfaction surveys, and who incur debts for their education that many will never be able to pay back. In 1964 Ricœur predicted that the progressive loss of direction in western societies would manifest itself on campus, and that it would soon spread from there into society-wide challenges to capitalism and to bureaucracy.

Ricœur's concerns of unrest for the university sector and for wider society were realized in 1968—the year he wrote the preface to a book entitled *Conceptions de l'Université* (*Designing the University*) (Dreze et al. 1968). By that time he had already witnessed rising tensions including the ten-day strike orchestrated by Nanterre students in November 1967, and the altercation between student leader Daniel Cohn-Bendit and government minister François Missoffe in January 1968 at the official opening of the Nanterre university swimming pool; in response to Cohn-Bendit challenging him on his apparent ignorance of male students' sexual frustrations (the student dormitories were single sex), the minister invited him to cool off in the pool. Furthermore, on 21 March, Nanterre student Xavier Langlade was arrested for taking part in an anti-Vietnam attack on the Parisian American Express office; in revenge for the arrest, Cohn-Bendit led the student rebels to occupy the Nanterre Senate Chamber. They stayed in that highly symbolic and prestigious space until 1.30 in the morning (Reader and Wadia 1993). So despite Ricœur's devotion to conversations for conflict resolution, Nanterre was providing a flashpoint for unrest; buoyed up by solidarity with worker strikes, sophisticated philosophy classes were not helping: the students were not listening.

The fragility of debate for resolving conflict became increasingly evident and by 30 April there was anarchy: led again by Cohn-Bendit, over a thousand students piled into a lecture theatre on the Nanterre campus, demanding freedom to act. Whilst over twenty professors demanded that the students be subject to disciplinary measures, Ricœur was among a minority of staff who strongly disagreed, encouraging dialogue. The Nanterre Dean, Pierre Grappin, decreed that the Nanterre campus would be closed as the situation was out of control, so the students decamped to the Sorbonne on 3 May and, when the police carted off the loudest provocateurs in the *paniers a salades*, ('lettuce shakers' being the slang for police vans with their wire grilles), the remainder took this as provocation and launched what would prove to be, completely spontaneously, the first night of the barricades (Dosse 2000, 461–474). On 6 May, eight students (including Cohn-Bendit) attended a disciplinary hearing which ended chaotically because the academics instructed to adjudicate felt they had no authority to issue punishment; the students enjoyed themselves at the event due to its surreal and inconclusive nature, which showed the futility of Ricœur's invitation to both parties to debate and negotiate. There were no structures for a different balance of power that might arise if the young demanded that the old justify themselves, instead of the other way around. After finding their elders amusingly impotent the students regrouped en masse: there were violent riots that night, with four hundred students and two hundred police injured. University towns throughout France erupted, especially Nantes and Strasbourg.

The Sorbonne was still under occupation and rioting was intense across campuses when Ricœur wrote his three-part 1968 paper *Réforme et révolution dans l'Université (Reform and Revolution in the University)*. First published in the national French newspaper *Le Monde* on 9, 11 and 12 June 1968, it offered Ricœur's responses 'in real time'. They show Ricœur's frustrations being tempered by a pragmatic wish to be conciliatory during an ongoing crisis for the university sector and for society generally. Ricœur argued within the context of 'the crisis' for more democratic processes that would enable students to have some say in managing their education. Yet his attempts to achieve this during the riots led to more chaos. Indeed, much worse was to come in spring 1970, when Ricœur lost control of the Nanterre campus; he was Dean when police were allowed onto the site. This '*banalisation*' (in French this meant opening the campus up to the law enforcers) exacerbated the situation and certainly created loss of trust in Ricœur's judgment from colleagues and students. On 4 March 1970, however, *Le Monde* published his Dean's letter (*communiqué du doyen*), in which he made it clear that the invitation to the police to come onto the site had been made very suddenly without his consultation, let alone agreement (Dosse 2000, 485; Ricœur et al. 1998, 34–40). The power of militant activism deployed by Cohn-Bendit and others trumped Ricœur's subtle dialectic—his philosophical interest at the time. Ricœur resigned from his post.

With regard to philosophy, Ricœur wrote prolifically and taught many courses in this time of post-war societal change from 1960–1969. His students, who were born during or after World War 2, were beginning to shape the world with righteous protest and the determination to speak truth to power, in ways that they believed their elders had signally failed to do by allowing fascism to dominate mainland Europe. We must also see the febrile world context in which they rebelled. Many French students knew about and regretted their country's and others' colonial actions and made attempts to demand justice: they recalled 1954 Dien Bien Phu, 1955 Bandung, 1959 Cuba, and the 1960s African movements for independence; they despised the French government's dealings with Algeria ('freed' in 1962); they noted the 1966 tricontinental conference which attempted to build an anti-imperial, anti-colonial coalition of Africa, Asia and Latin America and sought to use revolutionary means; and there was always Vietnam, where conflict was intensifying. During this period his philosophy reflected his preoccupation with good and evil, his increased interest in Freud and his ever-deeper investigation into the symbolic nature of meaning and the role language plays in mediating between symbol and reality.

In addition to full length philosophical analyses of human nature and morals (*Fallible Man* 1960/1965 and *The Symbolism of Evil* 1960/1967), Ricœur also wrote essays about history, politics and societal matters (*History and Truth* 1955/1965); he had, earlier, also written on Husserl (1949–57/1967). Of particular significance to this time of violence and conflicting views from 1960–70, are his philosophical Freud studies: *Freud and Philosophy* (1966/1970), and a more accessible sequel called *The Conflict of Interpretations* (1969/1974); and *Political and Social Essays* (1974), the last collection spanning writings from 1956–73. I draw upon some of these works because they resonate strongly with events that he was experiencing, involving communication, universities and higher education, as well as matters related to sexuality. In particular, Freud's belief in inner conflict (i.e. the deterministic structure of the sexualized subconscious as the determining and fracturing impulse of human motivation) was a feature Ricœur believed he saw in the students.

Indeed, as philosopher-witness, it seemed to Ricœur that one could actually attribute the events of May 1968 partly to a sexual revolution (Ricœur 1974a). Earlier, in 1960 he was attentive to the growing 'sexual revolution' facilitated by contraceptives. He contributed at that point to an edition of the left-wing journal *Esprit* called 'La sexualité' (Sexuality). He asserted that birth control makes it possible for love and tenderness to exist separately from procreation in a marriage, thereby making possible the perfection of interpersonal relationships. Yet he announced also that there are risks when 'Eroticism appears to become a dimension of leisure' (Ricœur 1960, 1673). He wasn't surprised when the male students on the Nanterre campus demanded access to the female dormitories. In fact, there is evidence of the woman's voice, although not heard much at the time of May 1968, becoming important and signalling the beginning of emancipation generated by the contraceptive pill and by gradually improved societal understanding of gender, sexuality and femaleness. Ricœur attributed the unrest also to the mixing of socio-economic groups (middle-class and working class, broadly speaking), which he wanted to encourage.

Broadly speaking, philosophically, he combined phenomenology and hermeneutics (i.e. perception of our world combined with interpretation of what may lie concealed). He attempted to contextualise the huge impact of Hegel in mainland Europe. Ricœur admired Hegel's contention that coexistence within institutional structures is necessary but struggled against Hegel's attempt to be all-encompassing.

5.3 Hermeneutics of Suspicion

Ricœur saw the human struggle to categorize the world into binaries also in the human use of suspicion: in European and American philosophy he is famous for developing the concept of the 'hermeneutics of suspicion' (Scott-Baumann 2009). Hermeneutics originated with textual analysis, but Ricœur followed Dilthey and Schleiermacher in 'reading' beneath human behaviour for motivations and meanings not visible on the surface of our interactions. With this idea he compared the ways in which Freud, Marx and Nietzsche made us suspicious of our own thought and action in the realms of, respectively, the unconscious mind, money and power. Descartes' belief that we understand ourselves because we can think and express ourselves with language, is fully negated by Freud's assertion that we are often unconscious of our thoughts and desires—and that we respond to them unknowingly in the form of impulses, verbal slips of the tongue and neuroses. This is often because of conflict between our desires and cultural mores, in some cases possibly but not necessarily from childhood trauma. Ricœur saw this insistent suspicion of human motives in Marx and Nietzsche as well as Freud.

Ricœur abandoned the term hermeneutics of suspicion once he came to believe that Freud, Marx and Nietzsche, the masters of suspicion, took suspicion too far in their wholesale critique and rejection of religion. He saw this as symptomatic of an overzealous, sweeping method of deploying a hermeneutics of suspicion: hermeneutics is based on the hope of finding productive meaning and contains the doubt created by suspicion, whereas suspicion is based on the desire to unmask apparent meaning as false. Hermeneutics would suffice. He came to see possibilities within hermeneutics to challenge meanings as well as to endorse them, which would render unnecessary the destructive use of suspicion. He hoped we could use suspicion in a way that is directly proportional to the situation at hand, which requires the ability to calibrate how suspicious one should be, and how to be able to trust oneself and others (Scott-Baumann 2009, 59–77).

Thus Ricœur (briefly, for less than a decade) deployed the term 'hermeneutics of suspicion' to indicate that we should doubt our own perceptions and experiences, as they may be influenced by unconscious emotional factors over which we have no control and of which we have little or no knowledge (Scott-Baumann 2009, 46); during this period, he watched students dealing with complex new freedoms, such as access to each other's student accommodation. Although Ricœur abandoned the term hermeneutics of suspicion, he retained hermeneutic practice in Freud's brilliant analysis of the unconscious and saw how it also relates to the existentialist assertion that we are part of the world we interpret, such that the self and its understanding of the other are interconnected: our attempts at hermeneutical interpretation carry our personal baggage. Freud helps to demystify our faulty and delusional grasp of truth, by describing and thus releasing us partially from our inescapable animal essence, and offering us more honesty than any religion, culture or historical tradition has hitherto done. Freud was the dominant influence upon Ricœur of the three; yet Ricœur baulked at Freud's determinism and excoriation of religion, wishing that faith, hope and positive thinking could be a better way than the negative.

5.4 The Changes Ricœur Wanted—Then and Now

To understand the idea of the university now in the twenty-first century, it is important and illustrative to consider what happened to Ricœur in the Paris suburb of Nanterre and its eponymous university, and why. His three-part 1968 paper *Réforme et Revolution dans l'Université* (*Reform and Revolution in the University*) was about the necessity of HE reforms, and was written with three specific goals in mind: first, to reformulate and update the idea of the liberal university; second to overturn old hierarchies by creating dialogue between liberal conventions and militant radical elements on campus; and third, to develop a permeable membrane between university and wider society. By 1971, after the Nanterre campus riots, he was arguing for acceptance of student politics on campus and a full understanding of demographic changes in the student body (age, class and numbers). He saw how the identity crises facing the whole of society (increased secularism, sexual changes related to the contraceptive pill, dominance of cultural mediocrity and continued elitism) were playing havoc with the very idea of the university as it metamorphosed into an entity that risked becoming either too dangerous in its challenge to the state or too complicit with the government. He also noted the increasing tension between the idea of universities as, on the one hand, the source of knowledge, and on the other hand, as training grounds for jobs.

Meanwhile the American and the British university system, although still elitist and sexist, already seemed to Ricœur to represent the practical approaches for which he longed: tutorial systems, smaller lecture halls than the Sorbonne, and academic staff on site available for one-to-one tutorials and group discussion. Across the Channel, British university students took a more aesthetic, less political approach to the change from adolescence to adulthood: they seemed on the whole to express dissatisfaction with the establishment through music, art and culturally eccentric self-expression (clothes, hair, sexual experimentation), and not through manning barricades.

Ricœur understood much French student thinking to be characterised by 'phenomenological distress' i.e. the self-doubt and confusion of not understanding one's own thinking (Ricœur 1974a, 1970); he thus felt that students would benefit from discussion and debate, not from revolt. Those discussions would explore, with some caveats, the thoughts of Marx, Freud and Nietzsche who postulated that humans cannot understand themselves because they are not in conscious control of their thinking but are controlled by financial pressures, by unconscious sexualized thoughts and by the power of others, respectively. Yet caution would be required since the hermeneutics of suspicion that they created (especially Freud) was too destructive with offering the shattered post-Cartesian cogito; student militant suspicion of authority was too blunt an instrument to resolve a wide range of motives including sexual frustration and discontent with a university education that failed to address real world matters.

In 1967, as French student activism was beginning to build up, Ricœur published *Violence and Language*, an essay in which he demonstrates the dangers of popular impulses clashing with hegemonic state powers, individual autonomy and the desire for equal co-existence. Violence arises quintessentially from an imbalance of power, and he saw this as an integral component of all political activity as part of his understanding that humans are political (Ricœur 1974b). The power of the state can be communicated via the law:

> The State is a reality maintained and instituted by murderous violence. Through this connection with the unjustifiable, the State confronts man with a difficult choice, the choice between two ethics of distress: the one assumes murder in order to assure the physical survival of the state, in order to preserve the magistrate; the other affirms treason in order to bear witness. (Ricœur 1965, 246)

In 2023, we see this violence manifested in linguistic features and violent actions that have become characteristic of the amorphous and hydra-headed political impulse called populism; being a 'thin ideology', populism cannot stand alone and is thus parasitic upon another ideology (usually liberal democracy) from which populism

5.5 Negation and the Feminist Cause   73

asserts that it feels alienated and apparently against whom it picks fights upon those considered less protected by law, such as Muslims or black people. Race attacks, murders and sexual violence happen under such a regime. Yet this version of populism in effect continues the work of the violent state, rather than attacking it as it disingenuously promises to do.

By contrast, the populism witnessed in 1968 France was what Laclau and Mouffe view as politically desirable since, as a movement, it engaged and united both workers and students in pursuit of better conditions for work and study respectively. The camaraderie between French students at the barricades (especially at urban universities) and the workers' unions was both powerful and pragmatic; together they believed they could rock de Gaulle's government and indeed they did; the protesters subsequently secured improved working conditions and better salaries for French workers. Ricœur's hope that such activism would translate into active student engagement with university structures at Nanterre was realized insomuch that students won the right to sit on management committees (*cogestion*, co-management). However, that hope was tempered with what Ricœur had predicted would happen (while he was seeking useful forms of collaboration with students through discussion in 1964): because of administrative bureaucracy, *cogestion* turned out to be somewhat illusory access to influence and students were left dissatisfied (Ricœur 1964; Dosse 2000, 374).

5.5 Negation and the Feminist Cause

Much has been written about the way in which the 1968 revolts in Paris seemed to be, and probably were, male-dominated (Scott-Baumann 2019), and yet, paradoxically, how these protests also made it possible for young women university students to begin to chart a course towards some sort of parity with their male counterparts. Soon after these events, Foucault would argue that sexuality and sexual difference constitute the dominant discourse of power in the West (Foucault 1979).

Ricœur lacked a philosophical interest in feminism or in questions of gender. My work on his study of negation shows his significant avoidance of, and actually even resistance to, any gender perspective (Scott-Baumann 2016; Uggla 2010). Denying the salience of difference is important also in terms of his conflicted attitudes towards identity which come to the fore in Chap. 6. Ricœur's views on identity allow me to explore in Chaps. 6 and 7 the tension between his way of thinking that accords equivalence to each and all in their capacity to suffer, to struggle in accepting personal failings and imperfections and also to enjoy life, and his refusal to acknowledge, indeed negate, the worse experiences of those specific groups (women, the disabled or those of colour) who have less access to the automatic acceptance accorded to the privileged (white people or the powerful). In fact, I will show in Chap. 6 that he knew we should all be, and yet clearly are not, equal before the law; yet he worried about special, specific demands for recognition that he regarded as specious.

By 1997 he was describing himself as following a 'sexually neutral thesis'. This suffered, he acknowledged, from 'the limits of a male way of thinking and writing'

(Ricœur 1997) and he accepted that this limited his thought; yet he believed that this lack of the female voice in the philosophy he was writing 'does not seem to me to require a basic revision of my sexually neutral theses.' As I have discussed elsewhere, this is a contradiction in terms: it is not possible to write in a 'sexually neutral' way and also follow a male or female or other-gendered way of thinking (Scott-Baumann 2016).

He did not see the gender question as a philosophical matter. I assert that gender must be both a political and a philosophical matter because explicit consideration of gender may facilitate the inclusion of the woman's voice.

In Islamic circles currently there are issues about participation, access to knowledge creation and status. Some Muslim scholars, usually male, are asking that women and their bodies should become active in 'Islamic public and intellectual life', as Khaled Abou El Fadl does; contrasting the dearth of women who are engaged now with the 'at least 2500 extraordinary women jurists, narrators of Hadith[1] and poets throughout Islamic history', Abou El Fadl pleads for the reemergence of women narrators of jurisprudence, actively and publicly engaged with law (Abou El Fadl 2017). In the Muslim world, Egyptian Zaynab al-Ghazali (d. 2005) was an anomaly in her scholarly activism (Abou El Fadl 2017); in his brief biography of her including her teaching and her torture Moazzam Begg echoes Abou El Fadl with his question for Muslims: 'In our homes, communities, and countries, have we nurtured societies and environments that could ever produce the likes of Zaynab al-Ghazali, or have we capitulated?' (Begg 2021). By contrast, in the secular arena of UK politics there are more Muslim women MPs than male (Chapman 2019), whilst overall 35% of MPs and 29% of peers are women (Institute for Government 2021).

In the western academy too gendered hierarchies endure, and this, as Shuruq Naguib's research demonstrates, extends to the coverage of Islamic Studies (Scott-Baumann et al. 2020; Ali 2013, 2017, 2019; IIITMedia 2017). The female exceptions in academia—Muslim and otherwise—can, nevertheless, help philosophers and theologians to focus on both women and men and to consider whether Ricœur's strongly dialectical, provisional approach can be of use in looking at the representation of women in higher education. He certainly perceived the power of human agency as well as humans' vulnerability:

> The openness of need by which I am wanting the world; the openness of suffering itself by which I find myself exposed to the outside, confronted by its threat, open like an unprotected flank; the openness of perception by which I receive the other; lacking, being vulnerable, receiving. (Ricœur 1965, 307)

The vulnerability intrinsic to such a statement seems to lend itself to the understanding of the 'other' about which he has written so much. Much later, in *Oneself as Another*, he wrote that our understanding of the other person is 'not only that of a comparison (oneself similar to another) but indeed that of an implication (oneself inasmuch as being other) (Ricœur 1992, 3).

---

[1] Sayings attributed to the Prophet Muhammad (pl. ahadith).

5.6 Ricœur Disappointed

Ricœur saw the university crisis as a societal problem: in his 1968 paper *Conceptions de l'Université* (*Designing the University*), he foresaw the risk if universities were to become defensive; he saw the struggles between republican and militant radical impulses as dangerous for universities. If societal pressure were to replace the university with something more akin to radical, revolutionary principles, this would significantly weaken the university as such a change would represent, in his view, cultural structures such as structuralism or Marxism untethered from depth of intellectual understanding. He could also see how impotent and perplexed the university becomes when faced with demands for recognition (individual and group recognition from students) without knowing whether such recognition would lead to increased participation or more standoffs (Ricœur 1968a, 16–18). At the end of 1971, when he had resigned his post at Nanterre, he spoke at a conference in Namur of the toll it took on him personally:

> I experienced at Nanterre the impossibility of combining nowadays the institution and this dream of liberty, and this is the heart of the drama and of the contemporary tearing. (Ricœur 1972, 548)

Yet I note that the 1971 paper reiterates the major point from his 1968 paper, *L'avenir de l' Université* (*The Future of the University*), which is an optimistic view in spite of everything:

> In spite of early failures [Nanterre] I continue to think that the university is a privileged location for leading the fight against bureaucracy, for sharing decision making and for inventing flexible new models of power in which spontaneity and the institution will be better balanced. (Ricœur 1971a, 73)

In the 1970s Ricœur was beginning to move beyond the hermeneutics of suspicion, gradually making his linguistic turn, which provides a more explicit focus upon the ethical responsibility that we have as language users. He incorporated into his philosophy the approach he adopted with students when possible: friendly discussion and reduction of the power differential, while at the same time being clear that the academic tutor, while knowing more than the student, needs to also learn a lot from the student (Ricœur 1968b, 381). He combined Kantian morality with Freudian hermeneutics so as to be able to believe that chaotic human instincts can become redemptive self-knowledge because of the principled and respectful way we can use language to search for truths.

References

Abou El Fadl, Khaled. 2017. 'In Recognition of Women'. Educational. *Khaled Abou El Fadl on The Search For Beauty in Islam* (blog). June 21, 2017. http://www.searchforbeauty.org/2017/06/21/in-recognition-of-women-by-khaled-abou-el-fadl/.

Ali, Kecia. 2013. The Omnipresent Male Scholar. *Critical Muslim* 8. https://www.criticalmuslim.io/the-omnipresent-male-scholar/.
Ali, Kecia. 2017. *Muslim Scholars, Islamic Studies, and the Gendered Academy*. Ismail R. al-Faruqi Memorial Lecture Delivered at the 2017 American Academy of Religion Conference. https://www.youtube.com/watch?v=ai5XF-bP3KE.
Ali, Kecia. 2019. The Politics of Citation. *GenderAvenger* (blog). https://www.genderavenger.com/blog/politics-of-citation.
Begg, Moazzam. 2021. The Tortured Scholar|Zaynab Al-Ghazali. *Islam21c* (blog). January 27, 2021. https://www.islam21c.com/islamic-thought/history/the-tortured-scholar-zaynab-al-ghazali/.
Chapman, Hamed. 2019. Record 18 Muslim MPs Elected, Majority Women. *The Muslim News*, December 27, 2019, Online edition, sec. Newspaper. https://muslimnews.co.uk/newspaper/top-stories/record-18-muslim-mps-elected-majority-women/.
Dosse, François. 2000. *Paul Ricœur: Les sens d'une vie*. Paris: La Découverte.
Dreze, Jacques, Jean Debelle, and Paul Ricœur. 1968. *Conceptions de l'université*. Paris: Éditions Universitaires.
Foucault, Michel. 1979. *Discipline and Punish: The Birth of the Prison*. Translated by Alan Sheridan. Harmondsworth: Penguin.
IIITMedia, dir. 2017. *Dr. Kecia Ali—Muslim Scholars, Islamic Studies, and the Gendered Academy*. https://www.youtube.com/watch?v=ai5XF-bP3KE.
Institute for Government. 2021. Gender in Public Life. *Institute for Government* (blog). May 7, 2021. https://www.instituteforgovernment.org.uk/explainer/gender-balance-public-life.
Reader, Keith A., and Khursheed Wadia. 1993. Women and the Events of May 1968. In *The May 1968 Events in France: Reproductions and Interpretations*, ed. Keith A. Reader, and Khursheed Wadia, 148–166. London: Palgrave Macmillan UK. https://doi.org/10.1007/978-1-349-22702-0_6.
Ricœur, Paul. 1960. La Merveille, l'errance, l'énigme. *Esprit* 289 (11): 1665–1676.
Ricœur, Paul. 1964. Faire l'Université. *Esprit* 328 (5–6): 1162–1172.
Ricœur, Paul. 1965. *History and Truth: Translated with an Introduction by Charles A. Kelbley*. Translated by Charles A. Kelbey. 2nd ed. Evanston, IL: Northwestern University Press.
Ricœur, Paul. 1968a. Preface. In *Conceptions de l'université. Jacques Dreże and Jean Debelle*, 8–22. Paris: Éditions Universitaires.
Ricœur, Paul. 1968b. Réforme et Révolution Dans l'Université. *Esprit* 372 (6/7): 987–1002.
Ricœur, Paul. 1970. *Freud and Philosophy; An Essay on Interpretation*. New Haven: Yale University Press.
Ricœur, Paul. 1971a. L'avenir de l'Université. In *L'enseignement supérieur: bilans et prospective. Léon Dion, Edward F Sheffield and Paul Ricœur*, 61–78. Conférences Perras sur l'Éducation 1. Montréal: Les Presses de l'Université de Montréal.
Ricœur, Paul. 1971b. Preface. In *Hermeneutic Phenomenology: The Philosophy of Paul Ricœur. Don Ihde.*, xiii–xvii. Evanston: Northwestern University Press.
Ricœur, Paul. 1972. Les Aspirations de La Jeunesse Namur Conference. *La Foi et Le Temp* 5.
Ricœur, Paul. 1974a. *The Conflict of Interpretations: Essays in Hermeneutics*. Translated by Don Ihde. Evanston: Northwestern University Press.
Ricœur, Paul. 1974b. Violence and Language. In *Political and Social Essays*, ed. David Stewart, and Joseph Bien, 88–101. Athens, GA, U.S.A.: Ohio University Press. https://www.worldcat.org/title/political-and-social-essays/oclc/253983933?referer=br&ht=edition.
Ricœur, Paul. 1992. *Oneself as Another*. Translated by Kathleen Blamey. Chicago: University of Chicago Press.
Ricœur, Paul. 1997. A Response by Paul Ricœur. In *Paul Ricoeur and Narrative: Context and Contestation*, ed. Morny Joy, xii–xiii. Calgary, Alberta: University of Calgary Press.
Ricœur, Paul, François Azouvi, and Marc de Launay. 1998. *Critique and Conviction: Conversations with François Azouvi and Marc de Launay*. Cambridge: Polity.
Scott-Baumann, Alison. 2009. *Ricœur and the Hermeneutics of Suspicion*. London: Continuum.

References

Scott-Baumann, Alison. 2016. Speak to Silence and Identify Absence on Campus: Sister Prudence and Paul Ricoeur on the Negated Woman Question. In *Feminist Explorations of Paul Ricoeur's Philosophy*, ed. Annemie Halsema, and Fernanda Henriques.

Scott-Baumann, Alison. 2019. The Values of Liberté, Égalité, Fraternité 50 Years on: Why the "Free Speech" Debate Makes It Even Less Likely That Mai '68 Could Happen in Britain Now Than It Was Then. In *Values of the University in a Time of Uncertainty*, ed. Paul Gibbs, Jill Jameson, and Alex Elwick, 217–28. Cham: Springer International Publishing. https://doi.org/10.1007/978-3-030-15970-2_15.

Scott-Baumann, Alison, Sariya Cheruvallil-Contractor, Shuruq Naguib, Mathew Guest, and Aisha Phoenix. 2020. *Islam on Campus: Contested Identities and the Cultures of Higher Education in Britain*. OUP Oxford.

Uggla, Bengt. 2010. *Ricoeur, Hermeneutics, and Globalization*. London.

Vinen, Richard. 2018. *The Long '68: Radical Protest and Its Enemies*. London: Allen Lane.

Open Access This chapter is licensed under the terms of the Creative Commons Attribution 4.0 International License (http://creativecommons.org/licenses/by/4.0/), which permits use, sharing, adaptation, distribution and reproduction in any medium or format, as long as you give appropriate credit to the original author(s) and the source, provide a link to the Creative Commons license and indicate if changes were made.

The images or other third party material in this chapter are included in the chapter's Creative Commons license, unless indicated otherwise in a credit line to the material. If material is not included in the chapter's Creative Commons license and your intended use is not permitted by statutory regulation or exceeds the permitted use, you will need to obtain permission directly from the copyright holder.

Chapter 6
Challenging 'Bad Infinity'

Abstract Ricœur enjoyed the open, collegial North American campus in contrast to the French atmosphere that he felt was characterized by student actions he supported, yet often understood as negative militancy. However, in America he also became wary of attempts by minority campus groups to replace discrimination with celebratory recognition of their difference. I interpret his approach as based upon a flawed understanding of power imbalances, exemplified in his development of the term 'bad infinity' to describe what he perceived as ever more insistent and insatiable minority demands. This is a common position that I see in myself, so in challenging his work I am challenging myself.

Keywords Bad infinity · Unhappy consciousness · Populism · Negation · Racism · Dialectic · Rawls

6.1 Negative Cultural Imaginings

What are the conditions for the possibility of truth? Is certainty of knowledge ever possible—especially since it is transmitted by language, which has ambiguity at its heart? In this chapter, I will use middle and late period Ricœur to focus upon how to avoid perpetuating Ricœur's misunderstanding of the mechanics of discrimination. I will show how his unwillingness to be direct about moral values regarding race and identity is common to many of us and has allowed the so-called culture wars to influence campus life.

Ricœur loved teaching on American campuses, believing the liberal arts colleges to be the epitome of good higher education (Ricœur et al. 1998). His first invitation to USA came in 1955 from the Quaker Haverford College, Pennsylvania—the same year his first essay collection, *History and Truth* was published. Over fifteen years later, after resigning from Nanterre University, he began a regular commute and divided his time between the University of Chicago (1971–1991), the Catholic University of Louvain in Belgium (1970–1973) and the Sorbonne (1973–1980). In America he taught many courses in English and published prolifically in French and English and other languages. It was also on American campuses that he experienced the student unrest and demands for recognition that made him uncomfortable about 'identity politics'.

There was considerable evidence of discrimination in the USA. In 1985 when Ricœur was commuting between Chicago and Paris, the General Social Survey (GSS) found that 55% of non-black American society believed that black people do not have the willpower or the motivation to bring themselves out of poverty. Such negative prevalent social attitudes would have made him uncomfortable; and indeed, it is disconcerting that in 2018 36% of Americans still held that belief. This is a large-scale negation of the willpower of others. In the UK the problem is less severe with circa 12% holding such views (Duffy et al. 2021). Such statistics make it possible to locate the negative in our cultural imaginings about race, because part of the populist conjuror's trick has been to hide racism in upbeat libertarian and nationalist free speech rhetoric. In the current culture war atmosphere, there is of course always a restrictive negative hiding inside an apparent right to uninhibited free speech for some but not for others. In 2022, a survey of almost three thousand British people found that 'being a man, being white and being a Conservative or Leave voter are characteristics that make someone more likely to feel that people take offence too easily' (Duffy et al. 2022, 4).

The foundational—albeit rarely discussed—negative that underpins these cultural imaginings is that the modern state often uses rights-based arguments to assert that it will honour the needs and rights of all, even and especially the most marginalized, while simultaneously negating this by asserting that such communities are more unworthy than they are marginalized; we see this in the government's determination to expel the Windrush generation (Gentleman 2019). The manifest negative binary is that black people are conceived of as 'allochthonous', outsiders and labelled illegal immigrants, whilst white people are seen as 'autochthonous' and belonging without question even if they are from another country. This binary can function as a cover to distort the relationship between the citizen and the state—a distortion that allows racialised inequity to go unnoticed by many white people until our attention is drawn to it—as Ricœur did in his 2010 *Being A Stranger* (Ricœur 2010).

There is evidence aplenty of this in the public domain to which we should turn our own attention. For example, the Wessely Report on mental health found that black people are more likely to be subjected to community treatment orders than white people (Wesseley 2018). These treatment orders can be extended to retain individuals in mental hospital for their own or others' safety. To compound this, mental health issues among black people are more likely to be caused by social stress such as racism, as opposed to being related to genetic predisposition (Bhui et al. 2018). Such inequalities are also evident in other areas of life. A 2022 Greenpeace and Runnymede Trust report found that black people are far more likely than white or Asian people to live near polluted land and dirty air and water (Craig 2022). Regarding women's health care, a 2020 report by MBRRACE-UK showed that black women are more than four times as likely, and Asian women twice as likely, to die in childbirth than white women (Bunch et al. 2021). In terms of the sociopolitical experience of British Muslims, in *British Muslims, Ethnicity and Health Inequalities,* the authors (who include medical practitioners and community workers) show through their research that Muslim religious identity is yet another explanatory factor—along with class, ethnicity, racism and deprivation—for the many negative health outcomes that persist for them (Dogra 2023).

Even though Ricœur abandoned his twenty years of work on negation (c. 1950–1970) as he settled into his lecture calendar in Chicago, in my writings I show how, after shifting to language studies, he incorporated his use of the negative into his language analyses (Scott-Baumann 2013). Furthermore, the original corpus of negation work also remains valuable for our understanding of discrimination and the way it sits hidden and festering inside the populist rhetoric of ethno-nationalism. In the only essay he published on negation, he gives us the solution: we need to *act*, rather than accept at face value the *form* of a negative argument. We can see this happening now, when polarizing and extreme culture war arguments demand protection of the current curriculum, the victors' voice, versus decolonisation of the curriculum. These binaries narrow our scope for taking action because they seem to preclude compromise and have an emotionally depressive effect:

> Under the pressure of the negative we must re-achieve a notion of being which is *act* rather than *form*, living affirmation, the power of existing and making exist. (Ricœur 1965, 328)

6.2 Whiteness

Yet action is rare. Those like me who do not suffer such discrimination are blissfully untouched by it and fail to take a stand against it, even when made aware of it by the experts on economic, educational, health care related, political and social inequities (MacDorman et al. 2021). It is these systemic cycles of discrimination that may be more deserving of Ricœur's epithet 'bad infinity/ies' (see Sects. 6.5 and 6.7) than the desires of black students on campus.

At least some of our inaction must be attributed to the fact that many white people enjoy more privileges than many black people do and thus need not change the status quo. This has led to scholarship and media noise about 'whiteness' as a phenomenon that must be challenged because it inhibits improvement for minorities. There are different ways of using the term whiteness: as a racial descriptor; as a way of analysing discrimination that takes place; as a value judgment because being white is therefore oppressive; whiteness as some sort of inherited privilege that is denied people of colour and whiteness as a bias blind spot (Malik 2023, 250–254).

There are many arguments raised to dismiss whiteness. For example, some can argue with conviction that skin colour is not the only discriminatory factor because class is also a major determinant of success or failure. Yet, ceding that class and poverty are also factors does not belie racism being the driver (Malik 2023). We could also dismiss whiteness by citing evidence of black communities in the deep south of the US wanting to be as tough on crime (and thus on black criminals) as white racists; indeed, one might even argue that black communities are racist (Jr. Forman 2017). That would however be disingenuous since it seems reasonable to believe that black people who want black criminals punished simply want crime controlled, and are not racially motivated. The criminal justice system uses the same specious argument, dismissing race as a possible contributory factor in criminal sentencing; however, their claim is debunked by statistics showing black people are targeted more by law enforcement and receive harsher sentences because incarceration is used as social control (Alexander 2012). What is required however, is the recognition that racism can contribute to poverty which can make crime a likelier outcome; the solution is thus large-scale social improvements to ameliorate the factors that lead to those outcomes (Alexander 2012).

6.3 Jim Crow

In order to understand the environment of the University of Chicago, I will briefly summarise some of the history of antiblack discrimination and violence in America. In the early twentieth century six million African American people were part of the Great Migration from the south to north of America to flee Jim Crow laws that discriminated against black people in all areas of civil life from 1877 to 1964. Chicago needed workers and attracted half a million of those migrants. Yet racism was rife there too: with the Ku Klux Klan well established and housing segregation enforced by estate agents ('realtors') and violent mobs, 1919 witnessed the extreme events of the Red Summer riots. Martin Luther King moved there in 1966 but was unable to make progress. In 1970, the American Nazi Party established itself in Marquette Park to fight integrationist attempts. Even in the twenty-first century, Chicago remains one of the most segregated cities in USA and young black people are still denied access to parts of the city with better employment prospects.

Amidst this Chicago culture, during the 1980s and 90s Ricœur developed a renewed interest in law and analysed the work of American scholar John Rawls, whose book *Theory of Justice* became a key text on the idea of societal equality that an egalitarian legal system could actualise. Rawls proposed a mythical, symbolic way of being fair by remaining ignorant of the state of affairs of those requesting justice: he thus proposed group decision-making from behind a veil of ignorance which would universalize fair behaviour in sharing social and economic goods fairly and avoiding selfishness: 'imagine if everyone were to act like me?'. However, the distributive justice that ensues from this procedure cannot, Ricœur reflects, resolve discrimination since it fails to create deeper moralities for resolving societal injustices (Ricœur 2000, 2007). In fact, the procedural basis for a moral code created by veiled group decision-making offers less than Kant's test of moral universalism; for Kant had already added community concerns and cosmopolitan issues to the person's load, the ever-widening concentric circles of right action from one person to many. Kant's moral imperative thereby demanded more than Rawls as he also enjoined each of us to treat people as ends in themselves, not as means to an end, and that it is possible to act as both subject and object (Ricœur 2007, 237). Rawls' focus upon fair exchange of social and economic goods has materialist features that neglect the need for deeper moralities. Ricoeur foresaw this in his early work on negation in which he shows the risks inherent in a model of conduct that relies upon having/not having. This can lead to delusions about debt/not having as a way to free oneself from responsibility to others. In fact, we are indebted to others in so many ways and these debts can be addressed by a both/and model, not an either/or dichotomy.

6.4 The Denied Negative Debt at the Heart of Authoritarian Populism

Ricœur's twenty-year long project on negation convinced him that we should beware of defining ourselves, as we often do, by lack, longing and loss rather than by what we actually *have* (Ricœur 1966, 23). This is the malaise at the heart of extreme populism: at its centre, I argue, is a potent form of lack—a nothingness, because such populism deliberately incites us to desire that which is unattainable, and which we probably at some level know to be unreal. For example: Can we really do without the European Union? Can we really have free speech? Can we change our gender identity fully? Are binaries real?

For Ricœur, it is necessary to accept that binary thinking is real in that it is an integral and irresistible component of much human thought; Derrida also shows that we often attach more moral heft to one of a pair, so that one is viewed positively and the other is negated (Derrida 1976, 2001). But, in contrast to populism's trick of insisting that irresolvable oppositional tension is the key to success, Ricœur demanded that we identify some sort of synergy even between opposed belief systems, since if there is no apparent overlap, such contrasts and comparisons would be unproductive.

Ricœur's lecture notes on negation span the 1950s to 1970s and demonstrate the disturbance to balanced thought that can be created by false negatives that, in turn, develop debt and debt denial. In his 1971 lecture script *Kant and negation*, Ricœur used several ways of explaining Kant on the topic (thanks to Goncalo Marcelo for translation). Of them, given the dominance of economic factors in our twenty-first century lives, I choose his economic example which shows the two ways in which the idea and concept of 'nothing' has been conceptualized in western thought from Aristotle onwards. The first is real: the cancellation of a concept by its contradictory concept, e.g. financial credit leading to and being contradicted by active debt i.e. money being lost (I had money, but now that I have lost it, it is not there any longer). This is real opposition: something is posited, it exists and is then absent. The second way is through a distorted version of logic that is unreal. Logical contradiction produces a different kind of 'nothing'. In Ricœur's notes on Kant we see this with the example of debit/money owed: when I fail to honour a debit note, I refuse to acknowledge that I owe money. In this second version of the negative, the consequence of one act (e.g. leaving the EU) leads to the contradiction of another reality (e.g. being in debt to the EU), and finally to cancellation of it and denial (I do not owe anything to the EU or to anybody; rather, I am owed) (Ricœur archives 1971, page 8452).

It is clear that it is this second type of negation (logical contradiction) that the populist rhetoric of the right (and left—see below) tends to follow. This is because the phenomena upon which the right-wing propagandas are focused (e.g. take back control, take back sovereignty, block off migration routes) are unsound because their use of language conceals unrealistic and contradictory states of debt. The impulse to leave the EU entails denying that we have a debt to the EU and asserting that we are not dependent upon them for trade, culture, history and security (our debit note). Although this debt is unequivocal, denying the debit note—and even trying to turn it into a quasi-credit note whereby the EU apparently owes the UK a great deal—has proven to be highly effective in rhetoric. Its success owes much to the assertions of lost sovereignty and the perceived need to support 'British values': they become so huge and ill-defined that they cannot become manageable concepts. The rhetoric is also deceptive in that the strong satisfyingly adversarial conflict it embodies does indeed promise a clear outcome: one 'side' will win the argument and the other will lose.

Left-wing populism also falls into negative logical contradiction when, for example, it takes a position based on the negative premise that leaders are by definition corrupt. The consequence of that is to free the worker or student of any obligation to the bosses, which is to deny any dependence on them; rather, we the 'people' believe we are morally in credit because we have the moral advantage as the downtrodden and we are owed power. This postulates a cancellation (our debit note is considered to be *actually* cancelled, rendered negative simply because we deny it). We can feel powerful because we have decided that we don't owe anyone anything. Paradoxically this powerful feeling is born out of the lack, longing and loss at the heart of extreme populism: it overcomes the doubts of those who may see multiple sides to situations, by implying that if they fail to support clarity then they are the drifters, the wobblers and the 'don't knows'; this accusation of weakness cannot be easily challenged. Thus, a high level of rigidity has become a marker of similarity between left and right extreme populism; and the terms 'left' and 'right' may have even become disorientating and less useful as markers of political positions and more significant as manifestations of extremities of thought.

At this point I propose we use one of Ricœur's several working definitions of dialectic to dismantle these populist binaries. He saw, as Adorno of the Frankfurt school did, that Hegel's dialectic absorbed the negative and thus denied us the importance of accepting negative aspects of our lives; nor I think, would he endorse Badiou's 2013 commitment to dialectic that is a positive commitment to communism (rather than a critique of it). Ricœur hoped, instead, for an iterative balance that gives weight to both the positive and the negative—and this is important as it will help us look at these apparently polarising strategies and make something positive of their outrageousness. Accordingly, both the examples of the right's idea of the EU's problems and the left's idea of corrupt leadership can be understood as rooted in reasonable concerns:

> Here by dialectic I mean, on the one hand, the acknowledgement of the initial disproportionality between our two terms and, on the other hand, the search for practical mediations between them – mediations, let us quickly say, that are always fragile and provisory. (Ricœur 1995, 315)

This method requires the detection, and balancing of binaries and is useful for deconstructing, taming and replacing with pluralisms those populist discourses which otherwise insist upon one certainty and drive wedges between groups. It is also imperative that we engage with the ideas we reject in order to better understand ourselves, since they will inevitably contain elements of our own thinking; indeed, Ricœur posits that understanding of self can only be achieved through understanding another person (Ricœur 1992). Teju Cole, in his essay *Black Body*, gives us a potent example of a Ricœurian approach: balancing binaries and being confident and positive, as opposed to measuring oneself by lack, longing and loss; he does so by rejecting the sense of exclusion from western culture imparted by his hero, the great black writer James Baldwin, eloquently asserting: 'Bach, so profoundly human, is my heritage. I am not an interloper when I look at a Rembrandt painting' (Cole 2014).

6.5 'Bad Infinity' and the Unhappy Consciousness

The Course of Recognition (2004) is amongst Ricœur's last works, so his ideas therein can be understood as reasonably final. In it, he explored further this issue of recognising difference in others, such that they feel content to be recognized; yet, Laitinen commented in surprise in 2011:

> There is really no discussion of the sense of recognizing one's identity, of who one is in particular (and not merely the fact that, like others, one is a capable, responsible agent). This is surprising, given Ricœur's famous earlier analyses of ipse-identity and narrative identity, which no doubt are related to recognition of oneself. (Laitinen 2011, 38)

I agree with Laitinen. Indeed, I believe 'recognition of oneself' is also closely related to the way a country understands its own collective identity. In Britain, state pressure is increasingly being used to differentiate people according to skin colour, while simultaneously denying that any such differentiation is taking place: for example, Ukrainian refugees are welcomed; Syrian and African refugees are not. Many plausible yet unsound sophistical reasons are given for this, such as that Ukrainians enter our country legally while people of colour do not. These legal/illegal options are fully controlled by government, and such an approach can influence individual citizens' attitudes. Laitinen follows this line with his summary of what full recognition might look like:

> the full course of recognition might be something like the following: i) recognition-identification of something as 'a something' at all, or as this particular thing....; ii) recognition-adhesion in accepting a proposition as true; iii) recognition-adhesion in accepting a norm as valid; iv) recognition-attestation of oneself as a capable agent, ...an irreplaceable person; v) recognition of others in the sense of esteem, respect or approbation or love.

And perhaps one should add the following: vi) recognition of collective agents, institutions, organizations, groups. (Laitinen 2011, 47 with elisions)

Given his work on numerous social justice issues and his excellent writing in *Being a Stranger* on the better or worse chances in life bestowed by being born into certain circumstances (Ricœur 2010), it is remarkable to note this omission of societal factors. Ricoeur abandoned his early work on negation which could have shown him that there are individuals and groups whose history of lack, longing and loss is inscribed so deeply that it can only be rebalanced with measures that destabilize his dialectical model. Is this perhaps a specifically French blind-spot of secular republicanism, where the society of equals cannot recognize its own particularities? The first French republic did not abolish slavery and subsequently, under Napoleon, the French empire maintained and increased its reliance upon slaves (Reiss 2013). Ricœur, in a section entitled *Multiculturalism and the 'politics of recognition'*, warns of the highly polemical character of 'a notion such as multiculturalism', and also names 'battles on other fronts, whether those of feminist movements or of racial and cultural minorities' (Ricœur 2005, 212–218). He analyses this as a problem of collective identity that is rooted in history dating back centuries and he worries that he cannot retain his 'descriptive' stance when exploring such issues (whilst in fact only spending a few pages on it). In an alarmed tone he seeks to define what is to him the non-normative nature of the politics of identity:

Does not the claim for affective, juridical and social recognition, through its militant, conflictual style, end up as an indefinite demand, a kind of 'bad infinity'? (Ricœur 2005, 218)

He believed this bad infinity leads to 'an insatiable quest', 'a new form of the 'unhappy consciousness', as either 'an incurable sense of victimization or the indefatigable postulation of unattainable ideals' (Ricœur 2005, 218). Here, he drew on Hegel's model in which the 'unhappy consciousness' is the third stage of self-consciousness after stoicism and skepticism; Hegel described it as trapped: that which '…knows that it is the dual consciousness of itself, as self-liberating, unchangeable, and self-identical, and as bewildering and self-perverting, and it is the awareness of this self-contradictory nature itself' (Hegel 1977, 206). Ricœur presented the 'unhappy consciousness' as the regrettable product of unreasonable demands for more recognition on the part of some peoples and some communities, thereby putting a certain level of responsibility—even blame—for this upon those who struggle in vain against lack of recognition. It is remarkable to note the growth of many forms of identity politics and attendant vulnerabilities: for example, the term 'trigger warning' was first used for soldiers traumatised on the battlefield in the Vietnam war, and now it is used to describe the misuse of words—as if they are weapons that wound. Such amplification of trauma requires careful attention. Yet the issue of racism is most urgently in need of attention, and we need to challenge Ricœur and move on ahead.

When reflecting on his decades of teaching in the USA, Ricœur offered this explanation of why American universities 'have never succeeded in integrating blacks in significant numbers':

6.5 'Bad Infinity' and the Unhappy Consciousness

> A large number of them [blacks] live in lone-parent families and are raised by single mothers; onto the economic disaster is grafted a cultural one. …. Blacks who have succeeded rarely involve themselves in educational activities on behalf of their own people; in this way the black community is massively abandoned to its own lot. (Ricœur et al. 1998, 47)

Using discriminatory terms such as 'their own people', Ricoeur's explanation lays the blame for the low educational attainment of black students on the black communities themselves.

This sounds like Oscar Lewis's 'culture of poverty' argument, i.e. that the values of the poor perpetuate their poverty (Lewis 1964). Lewis's argument has recently been reinterpreted as an argument that such values are not the 'responsibility' of the poor, rather they are a stigma created and imposed by the powerful upon the poor—a more Marxist interpretation. Yet the more recent interpretation of Lewis does not seem to fit Ricoeur's thinking here: he did not discuss causal and correlational relationships between racism or discrimination in society and on campus, or the possibility of institutional racism, and his arguments contain difficult tensions. On the one hand, he ceded that 'affirmative action' (i.e. the preference of a candidate representing a less privileged group over the application of a candidate representing the more privileged group) can be enacted 'by reason of the wrong done in the past—and, it is true, also in the present'; yet he also warned that affirmative action will 'explicitly contradict the principle of equal opportunity' by 'violating the principle of the present equality of individuals before the law' (Ricœur et al. 1998, 54–58). He was very clear that 'the paradox is indeed that the praise of difference ends up reinforcing the internal identities of the groups themselves' (Ricœur et al. 1998, 55–56) and that it would thus be better to allow the current legal, social, educational and cultural systems to take control of redressing inequalities.

Similarly, whilst he admitted that all are *not* treated equally in the law as shown in several essays in *Paul Ricœur and the Task of Political Philosophy* (Johnson and Stiver 2012), he nevertheless counsels strongly against the 'ideology of difference' especially when combined explosively with 'corrective justice' because 'the classical philosophy of individual rights is less and less apt for the demands that are supported by entire communities claiming an indivisible collective identity' (Ricœur et al. 1998, 56).

This analysis is shocking, given the high, systemic and systematic levels of discrimination meted out to black communities in Chicago during the decades of Ricœur's visits. The University of Chicago did not stand out particularly in the 1960s as a hotbed of American student revolt, yet the Black Power movement was energised by widespread and historically entrenched racial injustices, school segregation and housing segregation across the city. Mayor Daley's brutal policing policies only ended with his death while still in office in 1976; however, even after Daley's tenure, the university continued to implement clearance policies on black communities (Cohen and Taylor 2000, 183–215; Bradley 2021; Carlton 2020; Rolland-Diamond 2019).

The assassination of Martin Luther King in Memphis, Tennessee (April 1968) was marked by demonstrations and riots in Chicago and showed the depths of despair of black communities. When he left Nanterre behind him, Ricœur was in effect exchanging one unstable campus situation for an even more volatile one in Chicago.

As a visiting scholar without long-term institutional responsibilities, he will have been protected from its worst excesses, and he may possibly have been influenced by narratives from city authorities and lobby groups that depicted black communities as criminal. As Danielle Allen comments in her 2004 book *Talking to Strangers*, which she wrote while at the University of Chicago: 'Many in the university community believed the myths' of criminality adhering to black communities around the university from the 1940s onwards (Allen 2004, 177).

In the 1960s radical white students and those of Spanish-American heritage worked with black students to pressurise University of Chicago authorities into increasing numbers of black students and staff and altering the curriculum, with some success. But perhaps the most remarkable characteristic inherent in Black Power protest in Chicago was the students' conviction that these actions were not only about university issues, but were essential in improving living conditions for black and other communities beyond the campus. This motivation could also be attributed to the French students in 1968, because they worked effectively with French unions and workers to achieve improvements in labour conditions. However, the French movement was shallower, not deeply rooted in the need and the desire to rectify endemic social and political injustices such as those experienced across Chicago.

The Chicago students provide us with a template for encouraging students as citizens to see that they have an invaluable role to play in improving society. Their Chicago model of activism led to violence and deaths and yet, without advocating such desperate measures, we can take inspiration from the expansive democratic vision of students agitating for campus improvements whilst simultaneously looking outwards beyond the campus in order to guide, support and lead civil communities towards pressuring the government with specific demands for societal improvements, especially for black communities (Rolland-Diamond 2019, 364). Here Allen finds political friendship enacted, i.e. trust and shared resolve and goals even when cultural differences, for example, may be perceived as significant barriers to long-term relationships. As Allen expresses it:

> Political friendship does not solidify the boundaries of the community but encourages the cultivation of habits within the community that make cosmopolitanism itself possible as a cultural orientation (Allen 2004, 221, fn. 18)

Yet fifty years after the events of the 1960s and 70s which she describes, Danielle Allen notes with concern that the university had a private security company to provide armed response where necessary, and that this has since been expanded as a law-keeping element in neighbourhoods beyond the university (Allen 2004, 180–181). She accepts that policing the university area may have some short-term utility, but the long-term outcome has been the control and suppression of black groups since at least the 1950s; using the concept of utopia much as Ricœur explained it (see Sect. 4.6), she states: 'In my utopia universities would have no police' (Allen 2004, 180–181).

Because his discussion of bad infinity in *The Course of Recognition* appears in a section on *Multiculturalism and the 'politics of recognition'*, we can confidently accept that his thinking here includes ethnic differences (Ricœur 2005, 212–216).

6.5 'Bad Infinity' and the Unhappy Consciousness

Indeed, some years earlier, Ricœur had already listed 'sex, sexual orientation, ethnic group, social class etc.' as contentious issues on US campuses which involved, in his view, exaggerated demands for recognition (Ricœur et al. 1998, 56). He used the term 'bad infinity' in 1998 too, in his acceptance speech for the Kluge Prize in Washington DC, asking also how sufficient recognition could ever be received if 'the demand for recognition expressed in this struggle is insatiable' (Ricœur 2016, 3:295).

In his attempt to use dialectical balance that takes equally from each side of a binary with a seesaw motion and ends up, even temporarily, balanced, Ricœur's writing on this topic fails to take account of the sheer imbalance of power between former slave and master that cannot be contained within a Hegelian model of dialectical equilibrium. Rather, as Fanon explains in the final chapter of his 1952 *Black Skin, White Masks* ('The Black Man and Recognition'), for reciprocated mutual recognition between black people and white people to be possible, change on a phenomenal scale is required:

> I am not only here-now, locked in thinghood. I desire somewhere else and something else. I demand that an account be taken of my contradictory activity insofar as that I pursue something other than life, insofar as that I am fighting for the birth of a human world, in other words, a world of reciprocal recognition (Fanon 1952, 2008, 193)

Demands for recognition can be deflected by arguing that the ideology of difference can manifest itself in extreme forms that seem counterproductive, such as demands that only black academics can teach about black authors. However, an example like this can become a strawman argument, an exaggerated version of an argument designed to make it seem ridiculous, and thus easier to knock over than a real person would be. Here the strawman highlights an example of identity politics in such a way that it seems as if all identity politics takes such a stance. This is not so; many would argue the urgent need to increase numbers of black academics so that they can teach about black authors and avoid perpetuating the domination of white norms for defining black identity, while not excluding white academics. The strawman must be identified and dismissed in order to address and reduce racism. Ricœur did not propose a strawman, but he refused to accept that the norms used to discriminate against people of colour are different from the norms used to discriminate in favour of white people. He asked for 'equivalence without identity' (Ricœur 2007: 31, 114), and for a universalizable humanity in which we observe 'a just distance' (Ricœur 2005: 263). However, universalism cannot house the normative approaches he takes in his analysis of people of colour in America because they are racialized norms and thus different from those he applies to white populations. Thus we see how, in adopting Honneth's development of a theory of recognition using normative content (Honneth 1996), Ricœur excludes the possibility of looking at racism. Fanon was writing at the time of Ricœur's Algerian decolonisation efforts, yet Fanon described the individual and collective burden of colonialism in ways that Ricœur did not recognise forty years later in Chicago. Despite Jackson Reese Faust's argument that Ricœur and Fanon both sought 'mutual recognition untainted by racism or coloniality—a "new skin" for humanity', and can strengthen each other

(Faust 2022), there is a radical and ineradicable discrepancy in their respective understanding of inequalities. As Honderich commented: 'You who are reading this essay are, in all likelihood, a beneficiary of the system of inequality' (Honderich 2014, 19); indeed, the magnitude of discrimination is demonstrably one of the major issues of our time and thus has normative status (Goodier 2023). Fanon understood that magnitude.

6.6 Racism and Critical Race Theory (CRT)

Discriminatory practices can only be tackled if everyone involved in society believes that all people really are entitled to be treated as equals, and are taught this at school and university and by family. Efforts to decolonize the curriculum by using narratives from history's losers as well as winners are attempts to redress the imbalance in our cultural understanding of race. Yet, Kemi Badenoch, in her role as Minister for Equalities in 2020, argued against decolonizing the curriculum:

> the recent fad to decolonize maths, decolonize engineering, decolonize the sciences that we have seen across our universities, to make race the defining principle of what is studied is not just misguided but actively opposed to the fundamental purpose of education'. ('Black History Month' 2020; UK Parliament 2020, sec. 5.31.35–5.41.20)

In stark contrast, Kehinde Andrews argues in *The New Age of Empire* that racism and colonialism still rule the world (Andrews 2021): racism is not a new fake problem created by the woke; rather, it is *still* the defining feature of the longstanding status quo—and decolonization efforts seek to attenuate it. Although doubtless aware of the realities of racism herself, Badenoch seeks to discredit those who would reform the system to support global majority citizens and students. She relies on strawman arguments, repetition and hyperbole, i.e. the rhetorical skills that Gorgias and Callicles tell Socrates that they depend upon to convince lawmakers (see Sect. 3.7); indeed, her speech about Black History Month was delivered in the chamber of the House of Commons, which enabled her to make full use of the influence and power of her political status. Her hyperbolic description of critical race theory (CRT) as 'an ideology that sees my blackness as victimhood and their whiteness as oppression' (UK Parliament 2020, sec. 5.35.00–5.36.37) was praised by the editor of libertarian journal *Spiked*, who pronounced that Badenoch understands that 'the culture war is very real and needs to be fought' (Slater 2022).

Libertarians demand free speech and an end to what they call identity politics and the excesses of rights-based liberalism. However, like Charles Taylor, known as a social liberal (see Sect. 6.7), one of their main failings is their refusal to consider the reality for those who belong to a global majority of many different skin tones in which, generally, the lighter the skin tone, the more respect, more power and therefore more confidence and agency a person will be able to command than their darker-skinned counterparts, as shown in Phoenix and Craddock's research on colourism,

Black Men's Experiences of Colourism in the UK (Phoenix and Craddock 2022). Teju Cole also eloquently explains the predicament:

> There are glances all over Europe and in India and anywhere I go outside Africa. The test is how long the glances last, whether they become stares, with what intent they occur, whether they contain any degree of hostility or mockery, and to what extent connections, money or mode of dress shield me in these situations. To be a stranger is to be looked at, but to be black is to be looked at especially (Cole 2016, 6)

6.7 Racism: Can Ricœur Help?

Writing about the regrettable possibility of 'bad infinities', by which he means what he perceives to be the ever more insistent demands for recognition (Ricœur et al. 1998; Ricœur 2005), Ricœur failed us in two issues that concern racism.

First, although he admitted that equality under the law is necessary but may not be sufficient, he nevertheless found worrying, the exceptionalism demanded by some groups that represent a minority on campus.

Second, Ricœur was respectful of Charles Taylor's arguments in *The Politics of Recognition* (Taylor 1994) despite its implications. Taylor's anger about Canadian policies regarding the imposed separation of Francophone and Anglophone groups is instructive on language policies. By focusing on the way in which groups are identified by their cultures, Taylor was able to deliberate upon Eurocentric and Western values and relative judgmental discrimination against other cultures. However, of greater import is that Taylor's analysis functions as a displacement activity that ignores much more serious racial societal ills, such as long-term Canadian domination of the First Nation (the original inhabitants of Canada), as discussed by Glen Coulthard in *Red Skin, White Masks* (Coulthard 2014). Ricœur accepted Taylor's argument, believing it to be an effective critique of the argument that 'it is universal identity that appears as discriminatory, a form of particularism disguising itself as a universal principle' (Ricœur 2005, 215). Taylor inverted the situation so that those who are discriminated against with negative differential treatment, are actually depicted as those asking for unfair privileges:

> the politics of difference often redefines non-discrimination as requiring that we make these distinctions the basis of differential treatment (Taylor 1994, 39)

Ricœur did allow, adopting Taylor's dismissive term of 'politics of recognition', that this will lead to societies being judged in future by how they treat their minorities, but this is not good enough. The truth of racism is so much more fundamental, elemental and gut-wrenching than Ricœur or Taylor allowed:

> But the black body comes prejudged and as a result it is placed in needless jeopardy. To be black is to bear the brunt of selective enforcement of the law, and to inhabit a psychic unsteadiness in which there is no guarantee of personal safety. You are a black body first, before you are a kid walking down the streets or a Harvard professor who has misplaced his keys (Cole 2016, 13–14)

I imagine that neither Taylor nor Ricœur would disagree with this statement, and yet to support Cole requires more than agreeing with him. This common personal failure is incisively elaborated on by George Orwell in his discourse on a different manifestation of discrimination, i.e. anti-Semitism:

> what vitiates nearly all that is written about anti-Semitism is the assumption in the writer's mind that he *himself* is immune to it. 'Since I know that antisemitism is irrational', he argues 'it follows that I do not share it'. He thus fails to start his investigation in the one place where he could get hold of some reliable evidence – that is in his own mind (Orwell 2018, 44)

Similarly, people often deny that they are racist. As Honderich explains it:

> The agents of inequality are pretty well out of sight or, if they are in sight, they are ourselves, they are many and impersonal and they are distant from their work. (Honderich 2014, 37)

Yet if we return to Ricœur's interpretation of Kant and the negative, to assert that 'I am not racist' is to negate a debit, and to owe a debt to truth. Deny it and supposedly cancel it as a white person may, this is a refusal to accept that centuries of colonial, neo-colonial dominance and slavery by white majority nations have systemically and systematically reduced and are still reducing the life chances of the black and global majority populations in myriad ways. None of that is directly my fault but I need to acknowledge it and I can do something about it. Ricœur abhorred the facts of colonialism, yet did not see that the unhappy consciousness leads to repeated demands for dignity and recognition, and may be the necessary first step towards righting such systemic wrongs. If I deny all this I can only increase the negative by owing such a debt. Because I deny this debt it can never become a positive move that acknowledges transferred responsibility. By denying this debt I refuse to remedy the lack, longing and loss of centuries of injustice; one example of the latter in modern times is the bureaucratisation of state and civil surveillance of Muslim populations by the Prevent counterterror policy—a scourge Afua Hirsch explains well in *BRIT(ish)* (Hirsch 2018).

6.8 Communities of Inquiry Sample: Are Universities Perpetuating Institutional Racism?

> The government, the university sector and the media represent three current approaches to the issue of discrimination and difference on campus in 2023, which show how much the university sector has changed since 1968. As a way of exploring the approach of *Communities of Inquiry*, discuss these approaches. A group of 12–20 individuals can form three small groups, and each subgroup is to justify one of the positions set out below. Use procedural ethics to think clearly and stay calm.

6.8 Communities of Inquiry Sample: Are Universities Perpetuating …

The government:

On 27 June 2022 Michelle Donelan (UK Minister for Universities) advised the British HE sector to stop developing work on a 'race equality charter' because these 'diversity schemes' are expensive and they also threaten free speech:

> Given the importance of creating an HE environment in which free speech and academic freedom can flourish, I would like to ask you to reflect carefully as to whether your continued membership of such schemes is conducive to establishing such an environment. (Donelan 2022)

Donelan's intervention requests that universities think carefully about supporting diversity, inferring that there is no need to do so and that attempts to support diversity would damage free speech. This confused letter is difficult to fathom but seems supportive of the libertarian use of free speech, i.e. advocating free debate even if it is discriminatory. This implies that work designed to support high achievement of students who are different from the white, middle-class norm, is undesirable. Difference apparently does not exist. Racism supposedly does not happen. Privilege is clearly not a factor in success.

The university sector:

In response, Universities UK (UUK, the body responsible for supporting the university sector) asked for evidence to substantiate her claim. They asserted that they would not agree to follow her advice and proposed to continue supporting the sector in developing the race equality charter, asserting:

> We do not believe that free speech and voluntary external assurance frameworks are at odds with each other – rather they can help to address power imbalances and ensure a more diverse range of voices are empowered to speak up. (Adams 2022)

The 'antiwoke' media voices:

Alternatively, this dispute may be about rectifying an imbalance of what used to be known as 'political correctness'. It is possible that Donelan is responding to general alarm about the purported chilling of free speech in order to avoid upsetting minority interests on campus. This includes complaints (mostly from outside the university sector) about the muzzling of free expression though excessive use of trigger warnings, safe spaces and suppression of the importance of empire through decolonisation of the curriculum. The alarm can be summed up by the Telegraph article of May 2022 in which Sir John Hayes, who chairs the Common-Sense Group of MPs in the UK parliament, is quoted on the subject of this same racial equality charter:

> Be in no doubt, this is not merely brainless woke nonsense, it is a sinister attempt to indoctrinate students and to turn places of light and learning into places dominated by darkness. (Malnick 2022)

Donelan, the university sector and the media all say they seek to create *positive* and *inclusive environments which promote and protect free speech and academic freedom*. Donelan asserts this in the conclusion to her letter, and it is endorsed by the UUK in their response. It may, however, be necessary to consider the role of government and social media: are they complicating the debate in contradictory and disruptive ways? What do you think?

References

Adams, Richard. 2022. Universities to Defy Government Pressure to Ditch Race Equality Group. *The Guardian*, June 30, 2022, sec. Education. https://www.theguardian.com/education/2022/jun/30/universities-to-defy-government-pressure-to-ditch-race-equality-group.

Alexander, Michelle. 2012. *The New Jim Crow*. Reprint edition. New York: The New Press.

Allen, Danielle S. 2004. *Talking to Strangers: Anxieties of Citizenship since Brown v. Board of Education*. Chicago, Illinois: University of Chicago Press.

Andrews, Kehinde. 2021. *The New Age of Empire: How Racism and Colonialism Still Rule the World*, 1st ed. Dublin: Allen Lane.

Bhui, Kamaldeep, James Nazroo, Joy Francis, Kristoffer Halvorsrud, and James Rhodes. 2018. The Impact of Racism on Mental Health. Brieifing Paper. Synergi Briefings. Synergi Collaborative Centre. https://legacy.synergicollaborativecentre.co.uk/wp-content/uploads/2017/11/The-impact-of-racism-on-mental-health-briefing-paper-1.pdf.

References

'Black History Month'. 2020. House of Commons: House of Commons Library.
Bradley, James. 2021. The University of Chicago, Urban Renewal, and the Black Community. *AAIHS* (blog). April 12, 2021. https://www.aaihs.org/the-university-of-chicago-urban-renewal-and-the-black-community/.
Bunch, Kathryn, Marian Knight, Derek Tuffnell, Roshni Patel, Judy Shakespeare, Rohit Kotnis, Sara Kenyon, and Jennifer J Kurinczuk. 2021. *Saving Lives, Improving Mothers' Care—Lessons Learned to Inform Maternity Care from the UK and Ireland Confidential Enquiries into Maternal Deaths and Morbidity 2017–19*. MBRRACE-UK. Oxford: National Perinatal Epidemiology Unit, University of Oxford. https://www.npeu.ox.ac.uk/assets/downloads/mbrrace-uk/reports/maternal-report-2021/MBRRACE-UK_Maternal_Report_2021_-_FINAL_-_WEB_VERSION.pdf.
Carlton, Genevieve. 2020. How Chicago Became One Of The Most Racist Cities in America. *All That's Interesting* (blog). October 3, 2020. https://allthatsinteresting.com/racism-in-chicago.
Cohen, Adam, and Elizabeth Taylor. 2000. *American Pharaoh: Mayor Richard J. Daley: His Battle for Chicago and the Nation*. Boston: Little Brown.
Cole, Teju. 2014. Black Body: Rereading James Baldwin's "Stranger in the Village". *The New Yorker*, August 19, 2014. https://www.newyorker.com/books/page-turner/black-body-re-reading-james-baldwins-stranger-village.
Cole, Teju. 2016. *Known and Strange Things*. London: Faber & Faber.
Coulthard, Glen Sean. 2014. *Red Skin, White Masks: Rejecting the Colonial Politics of Recognition*. Minneapolis: University of Minnesota Press.
Craig, Mya-Rose. 2022. Why We Can't Tackle the Environmental Emergency without Tackling Racism. NGO. *Greenpeace UK* (blog). July 21, 2022. https://www.greenpeace.org.uk/news/environmental-racism-report-summary/.
Derrida, Jacques. 1976. *Of Grammatology*. Translated by Gayatri Chakravorty Spivak. Baltimore; London: The John Hopkins University Press.
Derrida, Jacques. 2001. *Writing and Difference*. Translated by Alan Bass. London: Routledge Classics.
Dogra, Sufyan Abid, ed. 2023. *British Muslims, Ethnicity and Health Inequalities*. Edinburgh University Press. http://www.jstor.org/stable/10.3366/j.ctv32vqmvd.
Donelan, Michelle. 2022. Department for Education. Regarding Free Speech and External Assurance Schemes, June 27, 2022. https://wonkhe.com/wp-content/wonkhe-uploads/2022/06/Letter-Regarding-Free-Speech-and-External-Assurance-Schemes-1.pdf.
Duffy, Bobby, Rachel Elizabeth Hesketh, Hewlett Kirstie, Rebecca Benson, Alan John Wager, and Jack Summers. 2021. *Unequal Britain: Attitudes to Inequalities after Covid-19*. London: King's College London. https://doi.org/10.18742/PUB01-043.
Duffy, Bobby, Paul Stoneman, Kirstie Hewlett, George May, Gideon Skinner, and Glenn Gottfried. 2022. *Freedom of Speech in the UK's "Culture War"*. London: King's College London. https://www.kcl.ac.uk/policy-institute/assets/freedom-of-speech-in-the-uks-culture-war.pdf.
Fanon, Frantz. 1952. *Peau Noire Masques Blancs*. Collections 'Esprit'. Paris: Ed. du Seuil. http://catalogue.bnf.fr/ark:/12148/cb32091544r.
Fanon, Frantz. 2008. *Black Skin, White Masks*. Translated by Richard Philcox. First edition, New edition. Get Political. New York: Grove Press. http://catdir.loc.gov/catdir/enhancements/fy0712/2006049607-d.html.
Faust, J. Reese. 2022. A New Skin for the Wounds of History: Fanon's Affective Sociogeny and Ricœur's Carnal Hermeneutics. *Philosophy & Social Criticism*, May, 01914537221090617. https://doi.org/10.1177/01914537221090617.
Gentleman, Amelia. 2019. *The Windrush Betrayal: Exposing the Hostile Environment*. Main. London: Guardian Faber Publishing.
Goodier, Michael. 2023. Black People Four Times as Likely as White People to Be Murdered, ONS Data Shows. *The Guardian*, February 9, 2023, sec. World news. https://www.theguardian.com/world/2023/feb/09/black-people-in-england-and-wales-four-times-more-likely-to-be-murdered.

Hegel, Georg Wilhelm Friedrich. 1977. *Phenomenology of Spirit*. Translated by Arnold Vincent Miller. Oxford: Clarendon Press.

Hirsch, Afua. 2018. *Brit(Ish): On Race, Identity and Belonging*. Illustrated. London: Vintage.

Honderich, Ted. 2014. *Violence for Equality (Routledge Revivals): Inquiries in Political Philosophy*. 1st ed. Routledge.

Honneth, Axel. 1996. *Struggle for Recognition: The Moral Grammar of Social Conflicts*, 1st ed. Cambridge, UK: Polity.

Johnson, Greg S., and Dan R. Stiver, eds. 2012. *Paul Ricœur and the Task of Political Philosophy*. Lanham, Md: Lexington Books.

Jr. Forman, James. 2017. *Locking Up Our Own: Crime and Punishment in Black America*. Illustrated. New York: Farrar Straus & Giroux.

Laitinen, Arto. 2011. Paul Ricœur's Surprising Take on Recognition. *Études Ricœuriennes/Ricœur Studies* 2 (1): 35–50. https://doi.org/10.5195/errs.2011.57.

Lewis, Oscar. 1964. The Culture of Poverty. In *Explosive Forces in Latin America*, ed. John Jay TePaske, and Sidney Nettleson Fisher, 149–173. Columbus, OH: Ohio State University Press.

MacDorman, Marian F., Marie Thoma, Eugene Declcerq, and Elizabeth A. Howell. 2021. Racial and Ethnic Disparities in Maternal Mortality in the United States Using Enhanced Vital Records, 2016–2017. *American Journal of Public Health* 111 (9): 1673–1681. https://doi.org/10.2105/AJPH.2021.306375.

Malik, Kenan. 2023. *Not So Black and White: A History of Race from White Supremacy to Identity Politics*. London: C Hurst & Co Publishers Ltd.

Malnick, Edward. 2022. Universities' Racial Equality Scheme Branded "Egregious Wokery". *The Telegraph*, May 14, 2022. https://www.telegraph.co.uk/news/2022/05/14/government-denounces-egregious-wokery-mps-question-worth-university/.

Orwell, George. 2018. *Notes on Nationalism*.

Phoenix, Aisha, and Nadia Craddock. 2022. Black Men's Experiences of Colourism in the UK. *Sociology* 56 (5): 1015–1031. https://doi.org/10.1177/00380385211069507.

Reiss, Tom. 2013. *The Black Count: Glory, Revolution, Betrayal and the Real Count of Monte Cristo*. London: Vintage.

Ricœur, Paul. 1965. *History and Truth: Translated with an Introduction by Charles A. Kelbley*. Translated by Charles A. Kelbey. 2nd ed. Evanston, IL: Northwestern University Press.

Ricœur, Paul. 1966. *Freedom and Nature; The Voluntary and the Involuntary. Translated, With an Intro., by Erazim V. Kohak*. Northwestern University Press.

Ricœur, Paul. 1971. Lecture 1: Kant and Negation. In *Unpublished Lectures*. Translated by Gonçalo Marcelo. Unpublished.

Ricœur, Paul. 1992. *Oneself as Another*. Translated by Kathleen Blamey. Chicago; London: University of Chicago Press.

Ricœur, Paul. 1995. Love and Justice. In *Figuring the Sacred: Religion, Narrative, and Imagination*. Translated by David Pellauer, 315–329. Minneapolis: Fortress Press.

Ricœur, Paul. 2000. *The Just*. Translated by David Pellauer. Chicago; London: University of Chicago Press.

Ricœur, Paul. 2005. *The Course of Recognition*. Translated by David Pellauer. Cambridge, Mass.: Harvard University Press. https://www.digitalricoeurportal.org/ricoeur-bib/s/drb/item/4202.

Ricœur, Paul. 2007. *Reflections on the Just*. Translated by David Pellauer. Chicago, Illinois; London: University of Chicago Press.

Ricœur, Paul. 2010. Being a Stranger. Translated by Alison Scott-Baumann. *Theory, Culture and Society* 21 (5): 37–48.

Ricœur, Paul. 2016. *Philosophical Anthropology*, ed. Johann Michel, and Jerome Poree. Translated by David Pellauer, vol. 3. 3 vols. Writings and Lectures. Cambridge, UK; Malden, MA: Polity Press.

Ricœur, Paul, François Azouvi, and Marc de Launay. 1998. *Critique and Conviction: Conversations with François Azouvi and Marc de Launay*. Cambridge: Polity.

References

Rolland-Diamond, Caroline. 2019. Black Power on Campus: Challenging the Status Quo in Chicago '68. *European Journal of American Studies* 14 (1). https://doi.org/10.4000/ejas.14321.

Scott-Baumann, Alison. 2013. *Ricœur and the Negation of Happiness*. London: Bloomsbury.

Slater, Tom. 2022. The Case for a Culture Warrior PM. *Spiked*, July 12, 2022. https://www.spiked-online.com/2022/07/12/the-case-for-a-culture-warrior-pm/.

Taylor, Charles. 1994. Multiculturalism and the Politics of Recognition: An Essay. In *Multiculturalism: Examining the Politics of Recognition*, ed. Gutmann, 25–73. Princeton, N.J.: Princeton University Press.

UK Parliament, dir. 2020. *Debate: Black History Month*. London: House of Commons. https://www.youtube.com/watch?v=ns2DbbwJ6cI.

Wesseley, Simon. 2018. Modernising the Mental Health Act—Increasing Choice, Reducing Compulsion. *Final Report of the Independent Review of the Mental Health Act 1983*. https://assets.publishing.service.gov.uk/government/uploads/system/uploads/attachment_data/file/778897/Modernising_the_Mental_Health_Act_-_increasing_choice__reducing_compulsion.pdf.

Open Access This chapter is licensed under the terms of the Creative Commons Attribution 4.0 International License (http://creativecommons.org/licenses/by/4.0/), which permits use, sharing, adaptation, distribution and reproduction in any medium or format, as long as you give appropriate credit to the original author(s) and the source, provide a link to the Creative Commons license and indicate if changes were made.

The images or other third party material in this chapter are included in the chapter's Creative Commons license, unless indicated otherwise in a credit line to the material. If material is not included in the chapter's Creative Commons license and your intended use is not permitted by statutory regulation or exceeds the permitted use, you will need to obtain permission directly from the copyright holder.

Chapter 7
The Politics of Pedagogy Leading to Polity Praxis

Abstract The free speech and culture war debates obfuscate and stop us examining difficult matters such as religion; we need to create a new form of activism, as I have done via the Influencing Corridors of Power project (ICOP) (https://blogs.soas.ac.uk/cop/). Ricœur's activism was in the word: he understood the full potential of language for grappling with the human condition. He believed that we must exercise our capacity to act to improve our world, bearing within us the negatives that we blame on others. I bring together here the three levels of word as activism: *Communities of Inquiry*, politics of pedagogy and polity praxis.

Keywords Westminster · ICOP · Political friendship · Sacrifice · Libertarianism · Religion · Community of praxis · Politics of pedagogy · Polity praxis

7.1 Transcending Binaries and Whiteness—An Outline

Ricœur struggled with the tension between analytical and continental philosophy. Though he sought to bring the two closer together, he found that they didn't want to be reconciled, preferring a standoff which strengthened their identity by being able to say what they were *not*. He thus developed a flexible version of dialectical debate to tackle this bi-horned bullishness that is also generally common in human thought (e.g. insistence upon male/female; master/slave; good/evil; black/white; Conservative/Labour); and his dialectical approach can be used to challenge the extreme versions of populism that currently complicate debate. Yet he failed to understand the horror of the black/white binary that determines destiny by skin colour and, late in life, he even distrusted attempts by African American individuals and black groups to rectify centuries of injustice by seeking recognition, respect and acceptance of difference as well as commonality. This bias blind spot in his work becomes a double blind because it is ignored by Ricœur scholars, which makes it all the more imperative that I act to challenge my own whiteness as the colour of privilege.

This shortcoming in Ricœur and in much of white society can be understood by taking another look at Ricœur's use of dialectic: he developed a powerful, flexible model of balancing opposing forces by seeking commonalities and reducing extremities in the way we interpret our worlds. This is invaluable for moderating our thought processes and also for understanding and deconstructing the current extreme populism of the mid twenty-twenties. However, this approach is categorically incapable of recognising and seeking to resolve systemic imbalance, which is vital if we are to redress the injustices of centuries. Ricœur was suspicious of measures that increase imbalance, such as reparations, and yet we must surely create opportunities that make individuals' success more likely than current probabilities permit.

My strategy to resolve this is to apply a three-fold model: three inter-dependent ways of exercising personal agency, using Ricoeur's faith in the power of language. In the analogy of Russian Matryoshka dolls, *Communities of Inquiry* (CofI) is the smallest doll of a set of three: she works to make discussion possible in all contexts. The larger doll she sits in is the 'politics of pedagogy', i.e. mutual learning beyond the university and with political engagement that reaches out into the corridors of power to influence democratic processes; this is the *Influencing the Corridors of Power* (ICOP) project (see Sect. 7.9). The largest of the three dolls is polity praxis. This describes the point at which the citizen exerts praxis by acting politically (not necessarily in terms of party politics) as a self-aware member both of the polity and of the political environment that governs us: this is achieved through All-Party Parliamentary Groups (APPG)[1]; the one I have set up with parliamentarians is the APPG *Communities of Inquiry across the Generations*[2] (see Sect. 7.10). I will focus in this chapter on the second (politics of pedagogy) and third (polity praxis) forms of agency, as I have devoted Chap. 3 to *Communities of Inquiry* and given several examples thereof at the ends of Chaps. 3, 4 and 6.

7.2 The Fate of Activism?

In the 2020s, various environmental, governmental and societal pressures have exacerbated societal challenges. For example, through the Public Order Bill,[3] we are being instructed to comply with political decisions arising from parliamentary processes, as opposed to being active, engaged citizens both in parliament through our physical presence, via our MPs, APPGs and other forms of advocacy, as well as away from it in our own communities. The bill has amendments that would allow 'the Government to criminalise a breathtakingly wide range of peaceful behaviour, including that with

---

[1] https://publications.parliament.uk/pa/cm/cmallparty/230111/contents.htm.

[2] https://publications.parliament.uk/pa/cm/cmallparty/230111/communities-of-inquiry-across-the-generations.htm.

[3] https://bills.parliament.uk/bills/3153. At the time of writing, it is at the 3rd reading stage in the House of Lords.

only the most tangential connection to protests' (Breen 2022).[4] If it passes as is, protests about issues such as cataclysmic environmental crises can be categorized as extreme threats to society to be suppressed, when in fact, given elected representatives' apparent unwillingness to act, it seems all the more imperative to be able to use one's mind and one's body legally to protest about the state of our planet.

Furthermore, at a grassroots level, the politicians who run this country often do not talk much to non-parliamentarians (engagement with even their own constituents can vary greatly) (Kuper 2022; Stewart n.d.). And in terms of talking to fellow parliamentarians, for many, non-cooperation with those outside their own party or even beyond their ingroup within their own party has become a principle born of the necessity to vote as instructed (Phillips 2022); this is a profoundly counterproductive practice for democracy. Another factor shaping parliamentarians' behaviour and the stifling status quo is the pervasive dominance of social media: so, parliamentarians are very careful not to be caught unawares with the 'wrong' person or message; and they—like public figures in general now—are less and less likely to discuss urgent issues honestly with those who may think differently.

7.3 Factors Militating Against Communities of Inquiry

The cultural imaginations of academics and their students are shaped considerably by the current parodies of the university sector as depicted in the media and some state departments. The sector is accused of being too left-wing, too free thinking, possibly even extremist; yet it is also reputedly prone to oppressive 'cancel culture' which seeks to protect overly sensitive students, who are dubbed 'snowflakes' since they would supposedly melt in the heat of challenge to their ideas and identities; they thus 'no-platform' those who would challenge them. In reality, 'no-platforming' (the institutional version of cancel culture) has not been used frequently: 2019 figures from Office for Students state that outside speakers were refused the chance to speak on campus on fewer than 10% of attempted bookings (Scott-Baumann and Perfect 2021, 44–45). The thought and behaviour of university staff and students is actually affected by counterterrorism policies such as Prevent that sow suspicion on campus and chill speech (Scott-Baumann et al. 2020), and the government-cultivated culture war, which denies the existence of institutional racism and the need to decolonize the curriculum (Duffy et al. 2021; Morreira et al. 2021). Compounding these are the two years lost to Covid-19, increased mental health issues, administrative overload, financial precarities, and, as Livia Scott notes, fractured, often barely existent staff-student interactions and relationships, exacerbated by Covid-19 (Scott 2022). Moreover, and overall, our society is weaker than it has been for decades, economically, socially and politically (Piketty 2022). All this makes it imperative that students and staff act together in a politics of pedagogy, overcoming their tendency to avoid talking to strangers, and using activism, knowledge and solidarity to step out beyond

---

[4] See also, *Sentencing Democratic Protest to Death* (Renton and Pandor 2021).

the campus limits to hold their political leaders to account, and provide them with ethical researched information.

7.4 Ricœurian Justice and Current UK Politics

In response to parliamentarians' unwillingness to engage with, for example, environmental and human rights matters, there has been a recent rise in demonstrations (such as those associated with Just Stop Oil, Greenpeace UK, Extinction Rebellion, Black Lives Matter and Free Palestine). This is in a directly inverse relation to the failure by governments to address these issues, matched by the British government's attempts to inhibit such protests through new legislation, such as the Public Order Bill (see Sect. 7.2). This state of affairs seems to place under excessive strain Ricœur's description in *The Just* that the social contract expects our leaders to act morally and deontologically, so that the morality of the act is more important than the outcome, as opposed to adopting an ends-driven consequential approach (Ricœur 2000). Indeed, in *Reflections on the Just* (2001) he admitted that this is not the case since Hobbes's vertical axis of governance and Weber's axis of domination centralize power and incline towards arbitrary exercise of power; the horizontal axis is Hume's axis of affection, which animates us as citizens and communities to try and live together (Ricœur 2007, 22; Ricœur et al. 1998, 39). These axes present a paradox: whilst politics necessitates attempts by citizens to live together companionably, it also makes it imperative that they accept leadership which centralizes power and which can be arbitrarily deployed against them. Ricœur did not believe that either of these axes could be dismantled, but that they must be accepted in an agonistic way, a way that assumes adversarial tension but avoids outright hostility between the two. However, Ricœur knew this prescription was unrealistic due to his experiences on the Nanterre campus: he described how he suffered 'unresolved conflicts within me between my willingness to listen and my quasi-Hegelian sense of the institution'; by this he meant that he wanted to support students' iconoclastic impulses while also believing, as did Hegel, in the need for institutions like the university. This conflict led Ricœur to 'the impossible dream of the hierarchical and the convivial; such is, for me, the labyrinth of politics' (Ricœur et al. 1998, 40). By contrast Jane Addams, with her standpoint epistemology, made extensive use of the idea of lateral progress along the horizontal axis, by leadership that involves seeking and meeting the goals of those without power and often with no clear goal in sight until it happens: 'Progress has been slower perpendicularly, but incomparably greater because lateral' (Addams 1895; Elshtain 2001).

7.5 Pragmatist Probabilities

To develop a philosophical understanding of the problems of race and articulate it to others, I first consider philosophical and then rhetorical pragmatism: philosophical pragmatism can be exemplified in the human mind as imagined by British pragmatist Frank Ramsey. His fascinating approach seems shaped by logic, yet surprisingly provides access to the human decision-making process. Thereafter, I will look at the mind and body as engaged with by Americans Jane Addams and Danielle Allen, both based in Chicago respectively before and after Ricœur: they both use a version of what Danisch calls rhetorical pragmatism (Danisch 2019).

In a manner that I believe is illuminating for understanding those who are routinely discriminated against, Ramsey redefined probability in a way that was acceptable in Cambridge to the dominant analytical (language) philosophers while using an approach that focused upon subjective perceptions more inclined to a phenomenological or even hermeneutical approach (although those terms were not common in the 1930s). In order to show how we gauge the likely probability of a situation occurring, he first analysed the classical model of probability as an objective and fact-based phenomenon based upon an example like tossing a coin repeatedly to establish the frequency of heads and tails. Given its distance from human thought, he consigned that model to the sciences (e.g. physics). Moving more towards continental type thinking, he then developed ideas in economics, mathematics and philosophy that are rationalist yet bear a close affiliation with pragmatist ideas, such as that our beliefs cause us to act in certain ways and the success of our actions can be seen to relate to the respective accuracy of our beliefs once we act and witness the outcome. He demonstrated how subjective our decisions about others and about the situations in which we find ourselves are.

To explain human decision-making, he defined probability as a numerical representation of an individual's *subjective* degree of belief; a prediction of likely outcomes based upon perceived possibilities and risks. He preferred subjective notions based upon induction, i.e. the gradual construction of an empirical argument based upon accumulated phenomena that are similar to each other and/or relate to previous experience. He argued that this model of subjective thinking is reasonably predictive of some sort of credible truth when it is based upon beliefs that seem to be often (although not always) confirmable by events: I will be in time to catch that train (and I did); I will be happy to see this friend (and I was); I have heard this restaurant serves good food (but it wasn't to my taste). His approach is characteristic of pragmatism in taking human thought and action seriously.

When belief, facts and successful actions coincide, it constitutes a happy coincidence that may allow one to see the motivating beliefs as 'true'. This can therefore explain a core aspect of pragmatism, i.e. action is taken both as an outcome of beliefs and also as a testbed for, as yet, unproven beliefs. Ramsey and the American pragmatists also accepted that a belief may be accurate but not lead to success, due to factors that intervene to frustrate our intentions; or that a particular (accurate) belief may not be appropriate for the chosen setting. Ramsey's marvellous work was left unfinished due to his tragically early death, aged 26.

There is also an important aspect regarding the amount of *personal* control that we have in collecting data to gauge future outcomes probabilistically—Ramsey did not stress this but I will adopt it to show why so many of us deny that we discriminate against people according to skin colour. I will show this by contrasting the probabilistic thinking of a privileged member of society, with that of a less respected member of society. Generally speaking, in Britain white people are more privileged, black people less so.

For many white people in the UK, the probability of success seems (relatively speaking) objectively safe, controllable and predictably in their favour. Class and gender intersect to compound privilege or lack of it: as many know without being conscious of it, white people are much less likely to be challenged, to be insulted, or to be blocked in their progress in life. By contrast, I imagine the person of colour may, thus predict being insulted, being ignored, passed over, not considered to be clever or well educated, or being physically harmed. Since they are more likely to be impeded in their life journey because of the colour of their skin, they may estimate personal success as based upon probabilities that are unsafe, out of their control and predictably and probabilistically weighted against them. Thus, the black person lacks the independence of the agent, the doer, who is white and makes probability judgements that seem objectively true (although they may not be) because the white person is more free to develop a range of testable hypotheses, relatively unchallenged by others. I imagine the person of colour may feel strong and determined, and may decide to ignore, to be assertive and to respond strongly to any impediments, but these are all demanding and tiring actions. Nor will the average white person notice that they have discriminated by acting 'unconsciously' in the pleasantly 'invisible' realm of unconscious bias and stereotype prediction. His own bias blind spot thus undermines Ricœur's 'imputability', i.e. the belief that I should be capable of judging the morality or ethical nature of an act and decide how to behave in the light of my judgment (Ricœur 2005, 104 ff).

7.6 Rhetorical Pragmatism

In his edited text *Recovering Overlooked Pragmatists in Communication*, Danisch argues for what he calls rhetorical pragmatism, based upon the understanding that people learn best through first-hand experience and through listening well (Danisch 2019). Listening to others with 'affectionate interpretation' of different standpoints is a creative act that involves conscious effort: pragmatism aims to explain the world accessibly from different standpoints and make it a better place, using action and language. With none of the concerns of Socrates, Plato or Ricœur, Danisch argues that we need to practice deliberative interaction using the clearest, most persuasive rhetorical language we can command in order to (as Allen would put it) form political friendships with strangers, i.e. pragmatic relationships with those who have different

7.6 Rhetorical Pragmatism

priorities from us and yet who can experience our needs by direct contact with us and help us to advance our specific goals. This experiential learning and such personalized practices need to take precedence over the pursuit of universalisable knowledge—such as that towards which Kant strove (Danisch 2019, 15).

A hundred years earlier, Jane Addams' centre for migrant women, Hull House, provided the location for such interaction, debate and research (i.e. *Communities of Inquiry*), and thus an opportunity for the politics of pedagogy in that she and her team worked beyond Hull House to act in the world outside. This led to the third and largest 'doll', polity praxis, i.e. finding agency in dealing with political situations and politicians to negotiate a better future in the public sphere. Her aim was 'to provide a center for higher civic and social life; to institute and maintain educational and philanthropic enterprises, and to investigate and improve conditions in the industrial districts of Chicago (Shields 2017). In Addams' words, this resembled a university:

> it [Hull House] returned to the people's lives and their lived experiences, instead of imposing abstract knowledge, and that emphasis on lived experiences made Hull House on par with the universities and colleges. (cited in Nam 2022)

The polity praxis at and beyond Hull House would have also embodied Danielle Allen's ideas of political friendship which she elaborates on in *Talking to strangers* (Allen 2004). Allen emphasises that equity is the driver for trust, and that trust can only be achieved when we know how to support group action and agree to communal decisions that may not always go in our favour, but that will benefit the wider citizenry—and also the smaller group with which we identify as individuals. By such means we may be able to develop what she calls political friendships, thereby understanding friendship to be a practice rather than an emotion. Equity, trust and friendship, however, are all bound up with a prerequisite: sacrifice. And this sacrifice may even have to be one-sided until it bears fruit.

Allen gives the example of sacrifice shown in the abominable treatment of the African American teenager Elizabeth Eckford in Sept 1957, when she tried to attend what had previously been a whites-only school and was driven back with weapons by soldiers. This sacrifice of safety and dignity drove Elizabeth's and other young African Americans' attempts to enact the desegregation laws; yet it required immense personal sacrifice since desegregation was vehemently opposed by many white people in their communities. Whites only accepted the policy once it became clear that desegregation was inevitable (Allen 2004, Chaps. 1–3). This example will be high up on a sliding scale of sacrifice; further down it, in their private lives each member of my team has been subjected to abuse and violence and felt the fear of being treated as less equal becaue of their skin colour or clothing. None of this sacrifice is acknowledged by the current political analysis of this country's situation or accepted as necessitating policies to protect 'minorities.' Instead, such sacrifice is mocked as part of the confected yet potent culture wars.

Danielle Allen's pragmatic approach of individual sacrifice, positive group response to such sacrifice, and practising human friendship could also significantly help to resolve Ricœur's fear of 'bad infinity', i.e. global majority groups' (often called minorities in race-rooted nation states) ever increasing frustration at the status quo and not being heard despite their ever intensifying requests for recognition (Ricœur 212–225) (see Sect. 6.5).

7.7 Religion on Campus: The Politics of Pedagogy

University, it has been asserted, is a secular space, and thus purportedly neutral; in a post-secular society, however, religion persists, and faith is often a vibrant feature of campus life. Habermas suggests that this creates a friction which places an onerous (but necessary) cognitive burden upon both the religious and the secular. He believes that people *are* able to recognise 'the limits of secular reason', and also that by virtue of that appreciation they should be able to refuse the 'exclusion of religious doctrines from the genealogy of reason', and thereby overcome the 'narrow secularist consciousness' (Habermas 2006, 15–16). Similarly, the religious consciousness, which does already respect 'the precedence of secular reasons and the institutional translation requirement' needs to continue adapting 'to the challenges of an ever more secularized environment' (Habermas 2006, 15). The ethics of democratic citizenship requires 'complementary learning processes' by both religious and secular citizens so that their respective mentalities imbibe the corresponding cognitive preconditions to engage in the 'public use of reason' (Habermas 2006, 16–18). However, Habermas accepts the impossibility of success for such processes. He decides, in a rather Ricœurian manner, that a precondition of success for a secular state involves the acceptance that these complementary learning processes are both vitally important and impossible to achieve: we will never fully understand and accept each other.

Islamic thought accepts rational means, but with recourse to *fiṭra* and *Shari'a*[5] as the overarching framework and guides; when considering the Platonic and Aristotelian legacy of ancient Greece, Hamza Yusuf elaborates as follows: 'the Sunni response was to recognize the great good in Greek learning but to place restraints on its sovereignty through a rigorous methodology that preserved the authority of revelation in its own domain over reason, while asserting the authority of reason in its proper place' (Yusuf 2019, 4).[6] I suggest that modern multifaith universities cannot expect their students to make arguments only through secular language, and that in order to avoid an excessive burden of self-justification upon religious students, there must be some accommodation in the classroom for religious thinking. Islam is understood to be the largest and most visible minority religion in the UK and thus it is remarkable that there is still very little accommodation made in the curriculum.

---

[5] See Sect. 3.7, fn. 2, and Sect. 4.1, fn. 1 respectively.

[6] [Cont…] 'The synthesis that emerged acknowledged reasons impoartance and place in the areas of natural science, mathematics and metaphysics rooted in revelation but maintained the importance of revealed truths unknown by reason alone. These were the two wings that enabled Muslim civilization to soar for centuries.'.

7.8 Polity Praxis: German Case Study on Religious Thinking

The British and American university systems maintain an attitude of guarded suspicion towards confessional Islam, whilst French secularism excludes it from education altogether. I find these approaches not conducive for democratic polities, nor for general understanding, and in a 2010 government commissioned report, colleagues and I proposed that active partnerships between universities, Islamic colleges and government should be fostered (Mukadam et al. 2010); regrettably, these ideas were not implemented.

By contrast, since 2010, the German state has adopted a policy of enlisting Islamic scholars and university support to address and tackle its concerns around deradicalisation, social cohesion, immigration and religiosity. Tailored courses prepare Islamic religious studies teachers for school work and to better support mosque activities, train Muslim social workers, and academically develop Muslim university intellectuals (Agai and Engelhardt 2023). This project, however, can be seen as a form of colonial governance (Hafez 2023), which is a valid critique that exemplifies a vulnerable necessity of the politics of pedagogy: whilst the project requires reciprocal learning and exploration of each other's cultural understandings and physical 'spaces', such as universities, mosques and community centres, nation states may seek to discipline and regulate the practice and beliefs of their Muslim minorities, thereby undermining their religious freedom and religiosity. This control over religious life complicates the negotiation central to the politics of pedagogy.

Ten German universities have become involved either with dedicated state-funded centres or with professorial appointments; in total about forty professors and eighty postdoctoral students comprise the current intellectual workforce developing the academisation of Islamic discourses at German universities. An emerging canon includes Qur'anic studies, Islamic law, Arabic, *Kalām* and Sufism, and there are also urgent requests for coverage of social issues involving Islam in Europe, such as gender equality and sexual diversity. The chosen German universities have to balance confessional issues with academic authenticity and develop suites of practical skills for the applied disciplines (school teaching, social work and mosque engagement), while also responding to alternatives, such as Shia Islam (Engelhardt 2021). This is, despite many difficulties, an excellent exercise in updating, interpreting and contextualising Muslim life within modern Europe to complement and/or challenge the efforts of Muslim scholars in society contextualizing their living tradition and its theology.

7.9 The Politics of Pedagogy: Influencing the Corridors of Power

UK universities should—but currently often do not—apply the politics of pedagogy, i.e. mutual learning within and beyond the university and with political engagement that reaches out into the corridors of power to influence democratic processes in what Jane Addams described as 'reaching our own ends through voluntary action with fair play to all the interests involved' (cited in Nam 2022). To help address this lack, in January 2020, I launched an initiative that I optimistically named *Influencing the Corridors of Power* (ICOP)[7] at SOAS, University of London. To achieve ICOP's collaborative goals in Westminster (see Sect. 7.10) our research team uses the politics of pedagogy: we started with little understanding of how Westminster works, but after much trial and error we now understand the various democratic processes that are available to us as citizens. In this politics of pedagogy we are using our twin understanding of models of learning and teaching and of democratic processes to build links between academics and politicians, thereby forging pathways between parliament and the university. And whilst academics and politicians are often quite hostile towards each other, yet individuals on both sides recognise the value of co-operation, and our work is an example of what Addams called pluralistic civic inquiry.

The strategy is for ICOP researchers to support academic engagement in politics in the following ways: track legislation, follow debates (e.g. via Hansard) and MPs (e.g. via Twitter), and keep pace with research from universities, think tanks and NGOs. The team decides in which live or upcoming issues MPs and peers would benefit from an expert angle: they plan one-page briefings, they commission them using in-house academic expertise, or co-author them with SOAS and non-SOAS academics, or commission an academic or field expert to write it. The team then disseminate them directly to 900 + MPs and peers via Mailchimp, along with Soundcloud recordings and they make both publicly accessible via the ICOP blogsite.

Through this mechanism, since ICOP's inception in January 2020, we have drawn upon the expertise of academics, lawyers, medical experts and activists and published over 65 briefings on a wide range of legislation and issues including: responses to Covid-19, free speech, freedom of information, think tanks, democratic processes, elections, parliamentary oversight, the climate crisis, counter-terrorism, covert human intelligence, health and care, education, Windrush, Afghanistan-Hazara, Israel-Palestine, China-Uyghurs, Tigray and others.[8]

Our briefings have contributed to parliamentary debate and resulted in SOAS developing its voice, being named and being trusted for collaborations. For example, in the House of Lords debate, Baroness Fox of Buckley cited approvingly from one of our briefings *Sentencing Democratic Protest to Death* (Renton and Pandor 2021) to argue against Amendment 115 of the Police, Crime, Sentencing and Courts Bill.[9]

---

[7] https://www.soas.ac.uk/icop/.
[8] https://blogs.soas.ac.uk/cop/icop-briefings/.
[9] https://www.theyworkforyou.com/lords/?id=2022-01-17a.1404.0.

7.10 Polity Praxis: An All-Party Parliamentary Group

The briefing *Policing in a Time of Coronavirus* (Faure Walker 2020) contributed to Abena Oppong-Asare MP's work and her report *Leaving Nobody Behind in Erith and Thamesmead* (Oppong-Asare and Beattie 2020). The briefing *Freedom of Information Needs Urgent Freeing* (Geoghegan et al. 2021) led to ICOP's first online 'open briefing' with parliamentarians, academics and journalists (openDemocracy 2021), which contributed to successful pressure for the Public Administration and Constitutional Affairs Committee to investigate Freedom Of Information failings in Government and across public bodies (UK Parliament 2022a).[10] MPs tell us they use our briefings as a basis for speech making.

To overcome the inertia and the knowledge gap about democratic processes in universities amongst staff and students, ICOP publishes guides, creates video explainers, and shares resources[11]; the ICOP team has also delivered several training workshops at SOAS in collaboration with experts. Through our efforts to engage in democracy, we have also learnt about and exercised various processes, such as the option of working with an MP to ask a question of a minister, which must be answered within a week; and we know that a well-timed briefing can help to trigger an early day motion, i.e. force a discussion of an urgent topic in the House of Commons chamber. Notably, we also trained The Ebony Initiative affiliates, members of a SOAS group which seeks to nurture the success of black scholars, and from whose talent pool ICOP also recruited a research assistant. Along similar lines, but at a more grassroots level, ICOP collaborated with Bollo Brook Youth Centre whereby young black students excluded from London schools produced a trio of audio briefings in autumn–winter 2020 on 'The Broken Social Contract' with extraordinarily penetrating insights into education, policing, and housing that were well received by the Education Select Committee and others.

7.10 Polity Praxis: An All-Party Parliamentary Group

A year and a half after ICOP's inception, in July 2022, black teenagers from the Bollo Brook Youth Centre[12] were part of the 90+ strong audience in Committee Room 9 at the Palace of Westminster attending ICOP's launch of the All-Party Parliamentary Group (APPG) *Communities of Inquiry across the Generations*[13]— a landmark moment in our bid to reach, engage and shape political conversation and decision making, and persuade aloof MPs governed by party whips to talk to us, to academics and students, to young and old, to communities and society. The

---

[10] Regrettably, the government subsequently largely rejected the Committee's recommendations for greater transparency (UK Parliament 2022b).
[11] https://blogs.soas.ac.uk/cop/training/.
[12] https://youngealing.co.uk/bollo-brook-youth-centre/.
[13] https://www.eventbrite.co.uk/e/communities-of-inquiry-across-the-generations-appg-launch-tickets-375532627197?aff=ebdsoporgprofile.

topic discussed by the six-strong APPG launch panel[14] on Monday 11 July was the Public Order Bill—legislation that requires the strongest possible challenge to halt the shrinking of our democratic right to protest and freedom of expression (Renton 2022). However, as Shami, Baroness Chakrabarti CBE stressed that evening, this constitutes just one piece of a raft of 'terrible' bills that have been passed over the past two years, and that continue to be proposed and deliberated; whilst ICOP's briefings have directly challenged the problematic aspects of many of them, far greater academic and citizen engagement is required.

As the secretariat for the All-Party Parliamentary Group (APPG), we (ICOP) are authorised, with support from MPs and peers, to enter Westminster physically and hold events. We can literally open the doors to those who would not otherwise consider entering; indeed, great excitement was expressed by the cross section of citizens who attended our launch, many of whom had never before entered this space, and who felt empowered and inspired to be more actively involved in democracy as a result of having walked the corridors of power. As we plan strategically ahead, the APPG will facilitate ever stronger connections with peers and MPs, and between them and the speakers and the public who we will urge to be active in the home of political decision-making, and outside of it.

Our utopia would be for all universities to have their own equivalent ICOP and APPG projects, and certainly some universities do already offer activities that embrace transformative research, fully engaged standpoint-based methodologies and international transformation of transnational issues, for example around migration, displacement and refugee status (Hammond 2017; Lambert et al. 2020).

References

Addams, Jane. 1895. 'A Modern Lear'. University. *Archives of Women's Political Communication* (blog). September 3, 1895. https://awpc.cattcenter.iastate.edu/2018/03/05/the-modern-lear-1896/.

Agai, Bekim, and Jan Felix Engelhardt. 2023. A Decade of Islamic Theological Studies at German Universities: Expectations, Outcomes and Future Perspectives. In *Islamic Studies in European Higher Education: Navigating Academic and Confessional Approaches*, ed. Jørgen S. Nielsen, and Stephen Jones. Edinburgh: Edinburgh University Press.

Allen, Danielle S. 2004. *Talking to Strangers: Anxieties of Citizenship since Brown v. Board of Education.* Chicago, Illinois: University of Chicago Press.

Breen, Maddy. 2022. Public Order Bill. *JUSTICE* (blog). May 23, 2022. https://justice.org.uk/public-order-bill/.

Danisch, Robert, ed. 2019. *Recovering Overlooked Pragmatists in Communication: Extending the Living Conversation about Pragmatism and Rhetoric.* 1st ed. 2019 edition. New York, NY: Palgrave Macmillan.

Duffy, Bobby, Kirstie Hewlett, George Murkin, Rebecca Benson, Rachel Hesketh, Ben Page, Gideon Skinner, and Glenn Gottfried. 2021. Culture Wars in the UK: How the Public Understand the Debate. *Culture Wars in the UK*. King's College, London: The Policy Institute;

---

[14] Excluding the host, John McDonnell MP, and chair, barrister Jacob Bindman.

Ipsos MORI. https://www.kcl.ac.uk/policy-institute/assets/culture-wars-in-the-uk-how-the-public-understand-the-debate.pdf.
Elshtain, Jean Bethke. 2001. *Jane Addams and the Dream of American Democracy*. New York: Basic Books.
Engelhardt, Jan Felix. 2021. Beyond the Confessional/Non-Confessional Divide—The Case of German Islamic Theological Studies. *Religions* 12 (2): 70. https://doi.org/10.3390/rel12020070.
Faure Walker, Rob. 2020. 'Policing in a Time of Coronavirus'. Academic. *SOAS Influencing the Corridors of Power* (blog). April 14, 2020. https://blogs.soas.ac.uk/cop/wp-content/uploads/2020/04/Policing-in-a-Time-of-Coronavirus.pdf.
Geoghegan, Peter, Jenna Corderoy, and Hasan Pandor. 2021. 'Freedom of Information Needs Urgent Freeing'. Academic. *SOAS Influencing the Corridors of Power* (blog). February 15, 2021. https://blogs.soas.ac.uk/cop/wp-content/uploads/2021/02/FOI-Clearing-House-Final-FINAL.pdf.
Habermas, Jürgen. 2006. Religion in the Public Sphere. *European Journal of Philosophy* 14 (1): 1–25. https://doi.org/10.1111/j.1468-0378.2006.00241.x.
Hafez, Farid. 2023. How Austria's new attempt to create 'good Muslims' ignores the majority. *Middle East Eye*. March 13, 2023. http://www.middleeasteye.net/opinion/austria-attempt-good-muslim-forum-state-ignores-majority.
Hammond, Laura. 2017. Livelihoods and Mobility in the Border Regions of the Horn of Africa. *From Isolation to Integration The Borderlands of the Horn of Africa*. Washington: The World Bank. https://openknowledge.worldbank.org/bitstream/handle/10986/33513/The-Borderlands-of-the-Horn-of-Africa.txt?sequence=2&isAllowed=y.
Kuper, Simon. 2022. *Chums: How a Tiny Caste of Oxford Tories Took over the UK*. London: Profile Books.
Lambert, Helen, Jaideep Gupte, Helen Fletcher, Laura Hammond, Nicola Lowe, Mark Pelling, Neelam Raina, Tahrat Shahid, and Kelsey Shanks. 2020. COVID-19 as a Global Challenge: Towards an Inclusive and Sustainable Future. *The Lancet Planetary Health* 4 (8): e312–e314. https://doi.org/10.1016/S2542-5196(20)30168-6.
Morreira, Shannon, Kathy Luckett, Siseko H. Kumalo, and Manjeet Ramgotra. 2021. *Decolonising Curricula and Pedagogy in Higher Education: Bringing Decolonial Theory into Contact with Teaching Practice*. 1st ed. Thirdworlds. London: Routledge.
Mukadam, Mohamed, Alison Scott-Baumann, Ashfaque Choudhury, and Sariya Contractor. 2010. *The Training and Development of Muslim Faith Leaders: Current Practice and Future Possibilities*. London: Communities and Local Government. https://assets.publishing.service.gov.uk/government/uploads/system/uploads/attachment_data/file/6155/1734121.pdf.
Nam, Chaebong. 2022. Jane Addams on Civic Education: Hull-House's Pluralistic Civic Inquiry for Egalitarian Relations. *The Social Studies* 113 (3): 137–152. https://doi.org/10.1080/00377996.2021.1997888.
openDemocracy. 2021. *How Can We Save Freedom of Information?* Online. https://www.youtube.com/watch?v=6ULUpwVLH1Y.
Oppong-Asare, Abena, and Holly Beattie. 2020. Leaving Nobody Behind in Erith and Thamesmead. *Labour*. https://www.docdroid.net/a9oUDSW/final-report-leaving-nobody-behind-in-erith-and-thamesmead-pdf.
Phillips, Jess. 2022. *The Life of an MP: Everything You Really Need to Know About Politics*. Gallery UK.
Piketty, Thomas. 2022. *A Brief History of Equality*. Translated by Steven Rendall.
Renton, David. 2022. Short Cuts: Swinging the Baton. *London Review of Books*, August 4, 2022. https://www.lrb.co.uk/the-paper/v44/n15/david-renton/short-cuts.
Renton, David, and Hasan Pandor. 2021. 'Sentencing Democratic Protest to Death'. Academic. *SOAS Influencing the Corridors of Power* (blog). December 13, 2021. https://blogs.soas.ac.uk/cop/wp-content/uploads/2021/12/Sentencing-Democratic-Protest-to-Death.pdf.
Ricœur, Paul. 2000. *The Just*. Translated by David Pellauer. Chicago; London: University of Chicago Press.

Ricœur, Paul. 2005. *The Course of Recognition*. Translated by David Pellauer. Cambridge, Mass.: Harvard University Press. https://www.digitalRicœurportal.org/Ricœur-bib/s/drb/item/4202.

Ricœur, Paul. 2007. *Reflections on the Just*. Translated by David Pellauer. Chicago, Illinois; London: University of Chicago Press.

Ricœur, Paul, François Azouvi, and Marc de Launay. 1998. *Critique and Conviction: Conversations with François Azouvi and Marc de Launay*. Cambridge: Polity.

Scott, Livia. 2022. 'Why Won't Students Talk to Staff?' Higher Education Policy. *Wonkhe* (blog). July 22, 2022. https://wonkhe.com/blogs/why-wont-students-talk-to-staff/.

Scott-Baumann, Alison, and Simon Perfect. 2021. *Freedom of Speech in Universities Islam, Charities and Counter-Terrorism*. Islam in the World. London & New York: Routledge, Taylor & Francis Group.

Scott-Baumann, Alison, Sariya Cheruvallil-Contractor, Shuruq Naguib, Mathew Guest, and Aisha Phoenix. 2020. *Islam on Campus: Contested Identities and the Cultures of Higher Education in Britain*. OUP Oxford.

Shields, Patricia, ed. 2017. *Jane Addams: Progressive Pioneer of Peace, Philosophy, Sociology, Social Work and Public Administration: 10*. 1st ed. 2017 edition. New York, NY: Springer.

Stewart, Rory. n.d. 'Synthesis'. Audio. The Long History of Argument—From Socrates to Social Media. Accessed July 28, 2022. https://www.bbc.co.uk/sounds/play/m0019rj2.

UK Parliament. 2022a. '"Poor" Handling of FOI Requests by Government Spurs Call for Independent Audit'. UK Parliament. *Committees* (blog). April 29, 2022a. https://committees.parliament.uk/committee/327/public-administration-and-constitutional-affairs-committee/news/166107/poor-handling-of-foi-requests-by-government-spurs-call-for-independent-audit/.

UK Parliament. 2022b. 'Cabinet Office Rejects Recommendations to Improve Transparency of Its FOI Handling'. UK Parliament. *Committees* (blog). July 7, 2022b. https://committees.parliament.uk/committee/327/public-administration-and-constitutional-affairs-committee/news/171927/cabinet-office-rejects-recommendations-to-improve-transparency-of-its-foi-handling/.

Yusuf, Hamza. 2019. Medina and Athena: Restoring a Lost Legacy. *Renovatio: How Do We Know?* 3 (1): 1–12.

Open Access This chapter is licensed under the terms of the Creative Commons Attribution 4.0 International License (http://creativecommons.org/licenses/by/4.0/), which permits use, sharing, adaptation, distribution and reproduction in any medium or format, as long as you give appropriate credit to the original author(s) and the source, provide a link to the Creative Commons license and indicate if changes were made.

The images or other third party material in this chapter are included in the chapter's Creative Commons license, unless indicated otherwise in a credit line to the material. If material is not included in the chapter's Creative Commons license and your intended use is not permitted by statutory regulation or exceeds the permitted use, you will need to obtain permission directly from the copyright holder.

Chapter 8
Conclusion

Abstract Ricoeur's philosophy offers great strengths by insisting upon the value of discussion for building a better world, particularly through improving the university sector. His model of higher education reform is even more relevant now and his dialectical model of delicate, provisional balancing of different views proves useful for analyzing and challenging populist binaries. Yet this dialectical model is inadequate for redressing gross societal imbalances created and perpetuated by the concept of race and the practice of racism. Here I summarise the problems and possible practical solutions I am enacting, and make broader recommendations for the UK's university sector.

Keywords APPG · Binaries · *Communities of Inquiry* · Culture wars · Dialectics · Discrimination · ICOP · Free speech · Racism · Westminster

Paul Ricœur understood that he was a man of words: 'The word is my kingdom, and I am not ashamed of it'. Yet he also qualified this due to the societal shame he experienced: 'to the extent that my speaking shares in the guilt of an unjust society which exploits work' (Ricœur 1965, 5).

With this burden, he created his own autobiographical style that features a trifocal lens: exploration of his own identity ran parallel with both a universal narrative and a historical analysis. He wrote of the incompletion of our experiences, the corruption of governments, the violence of the state and the bruised cogito that characterises the modern human's existence. By an accident of birth, he had the privilege of the white male, an advantage that is invisible to those who have it.

His work is deeply moral. And it has a powerful immediacy too, relevant to the twenty-first century: Ricoeur stood *against* colonialism and fascism, and *for* a common European identity. He strove for educational practices that were inclusive and worked towards identity based on acceptance of the contradictory destructive and self-destructive aspects of every individual. We can take inspiration from this approach, helping us to understand his response to the Algerian crisis of the 1950s and early 1960s, and why this inspired the university students he stood alongside.

His insistence upon our ethical responsibility to use language powerfully yet compassionately is invaluable for using language to work together. His insistence upon balancing debate is invaluable for deconstructing the extremisms of populist binaries. Over time however, his normative approach to a philosophy of values became more distant from his youthful attempts to meet students' demands for self-determination. This conflicted with the identity struggles of underprivileged groups in the 1980s in the USA, which he found unreasonable. We need a different approach if we want to rebalance historical wrongs that currently still distort the rights and dignity of all, regardless of skin colour.

In terms of free speech, having entrenched ourselves into negative ways of thinking, our ability to communicate well has been inhibited: 'You can't say that' is a common refrain and taking offence is now a characteristic response to the comments and actions of others. In Ricœur's kingdom of the word this is unacceptable (Ricœur 1965, 5), and through Ricœurian analysis of the structure and content of language and of philosophy we can relearn how to communicate well; we can deconstruct the binaries that we are presented with and manipulated by, and we can approach our use of language as an ethical wager that we make with ourselves and others in order to be fair to each other.

Yet this wager requires more than Ricœur envisaged, as trends such as culture wars, the woke debate and opposition to the decolonising agenda (to name just three) are much more exaggerated in their use of emotion and untruths than anything he experienced, even in his Chicago days. His desire to differentiate between action and passion, which he called opposites, cannot be maintained in this current climate of structural racism and legitimized bigotry (Ricœur 2007). We need to engage emotionally as well as cerebrally.

The three urgent moves he proposed in 1968 in his preface to *Conceptions de l'université* (*Designing the University*) are still urgent for reformulating the idea of the university. He wanted somehow to create a permeable membrane between the university and society. First, he proposed to help students understand better higher education's utilitarian impulses to prepare them for the job marketplace—then they can make job *and other* choices; secondly to insist upon full student participation in policymaking in the running of the university; and thirdly, to help students challenge modern consumerist culture and communicate effectively with the outside world by engaging directly (Ricœur 1968). He found this difficult on the Chicago campus.

Both Jane Addams and Danielle Allen provide a rich, more capacious and pragmatic vision of Chicago than Ricœur's. Jane Addams (little known until comparatively recently) gives us an early and invaluable version of standpoint thinking: knowledge creation and the practice of working in groups are context based, gender related and subjective. The *Communities of Inquiry* approach, by creating a group that formulates procedural ethics, allows us to develop group solidarity, to have agency as individuals and to work together to make practical decisions that can be implemented for the benefit of the wider community—as Addams did by bringing refugees, researchers and politicians together.

In our attempts to work together we must be conscious of the language we use: Aristotle listed cases of abusive language as examples of wrongs committed. I find this fits our current societal dilemmas: in the cultural imagination of our modern liberal democracy, we have recently come to believe that others will use abusive language to be offensive to us. This fear of causing the anticipated offence, amplified by social media, is one major factor in people's tendency to speak less about complex topics—seen in the common current tendency to react negatively to comments *as if* they are meant as insults. To counter this we must attempt equity: 'Equity is friendship's core' and is determined by ethical reciprocity (Allen 2004, 129). In *Communities of Inquiry* this can be achieved by using the approaches discussed in Chap. 3 which show how friendship and group bonds can be the model for conversation in pairs and groups, and which address and displace offence and suspicion.

In the 2020s, the higher education sector in the UK has become enmeshed in complex, aggressive arguments about identity, nationality and race. These arguments have become intensely negative and politicised, when government places the university under attack for its perceived adherence to liberal secular ideas. These ideas are believed by certain voices in the government to be antipathetic to the more libertarian secular values represented by government. This seems like a non-debate that could easily be cleared up; yet instead, it has escalated into persecution of universities under the ideological guise of so-called culture wars that invoke ethnonationalism and xenophobia. Recent attempts by the Home Office to reduce numbers of foreign students is part of the xenophobic desire to reduce immigration, which will also deprive universities of the intellects and the money they need (Ward-Glenton 2022). While the university sector fails to defend itself or make the case for debate, instead seeking to accommodate the arguments brought against it by government, the education secretary Gillian Keegan is locked in a sort of culture war with the Home Office in her quest to bring in more foreign students (Taylor 2023). This book captures a moment in time that is a shameful demonstration of bad binary rhetoric.

The university sector seems paralysed in the pincer grip from right-wing libertarians off campus and left-wing no-platformers on campus: each side influences the other to press harder and be more extreme. In order to counter these immediate pressures, we need to begin by visualizing the university as a space where the power of speech must hold its ground, whilst responsibly and effectively managing the most objectionable forms of speech. Furthermore, to also resist the neoliberal demands of government to monetize higher education, the university system needs to govern itself by participatory democratic methods and be overseen by an independent regulator. Most importantly, students and staff need to decline urgently the 'divide and rule' culture wars that enmesh them in inactivity, and consider how to emulate the flawed yet necessary Chicago activists' commitment both to campus matters and to the wider community.

Through the *Influencing Corridors of Power* project, and the *All-Party Parliamentary Group,* we have stepped aside from the spider's web of free speech discourse that entraps and distracts, to create a fresh space and a more informed activism and to bring expert opinion to bear on events in Westminster that affect us all (see Chap. 7). Academic university experts, legal and medical experts beyond academia, and activist groups and think tanks are providing us with information. The networks we have collectively built with parliamentarians are reducing the democratic deficit, the ignorance of many students, academics and even parliamentarians about democratic processes by giving access to these processes. Indeed, this is happening already, but the free speech narratives have quieted the university sector's confidence and we need to speak again. The ICOP journey began with an acceptance that we knew very little about Westminster and would make progress only by being comfortable with mistakes, trial and error and failure. And at all levels—parliamentary, university, society, family—we have to overcome the tension created by the free speech and culture wars and make a conscious effort to negotiate our different truths, sitting together, co-present in fragile trust and with the openly shared risk of offending each other, for which we will apologise, seeking to understand that ways of thinking may work in some situations and not in others. Ricoeur's dialectical model is invaluable for challenging the extreme populist binaries that seek to divide us. However, we need to also accept the urgent need to redistribute privilege in ways that unbalance Ricoeur's dialectics by addressing the bias blind spot that allows discrimination.

In terms of the issues I have analysed in this book, I urge all involved in the university sector to:

1. contextualise and clarify current campus developments by comparison and contrast with other systems or historical versions (see Chaps. 4 and 5)
2. use different disciplines (in my case, philosophy) to better understand state interventions in higher education (see Chaps. 1–7)
3. learn how to recognize and challenge systemic 'structural racism', especially in its recent disguises as counter terrorism, anti-wokeness, culture wars and free speech wars (see Chaps. 1, 2 and 4)
4. labour to replace it with positive policies for social change, including accountability for racial and cultural inclusion (see Chaps. 6 and 7)
5. focus upon access and attainment disparities, programmatic and curricular reviews, and thereby transform programmes into multidisciplinary, decolonized, culturally sensitive learning and teaching (see the work of Dr. Awino Okech at SOAS, University of London, Dr. Paul Campbell at the University of Leicester, and Dr. Barbara Adewumi and Rachel Gefferie at the University of Kent)
6. develop an institutional atmosphere that facilitates good, open debate and avoids no-platforming (see Chaps. 3 and 7)
7. ensure that terms such as 'institutional racism' are used frequently and have productive discussions to eliminate Islamophobia and racial discrimination against black staff and students, and those of colour (see Chaps. 1, 2 and 6)
8. create opportunities for *Communities of Inquiry*, politics of pedagogy and polity praxis, so that the university can fulfil its societal commitment to its own staff and students and to the wider world, including government (see Chap. 7)
9. in our current state of cultural confusion, online manipulation and environmental disaster, the university sector must more bravely capitalize on its unique capacity to be pragmatist, to speak out and engage more assertively with the populist binaries that divide us (see Chaps. 3, 7 and 8)
10. deploy all the above to address discrimination of all kinds.

In the end, as current Director of the School of Oriental and African Studies, University of London Adam Habib shows in his book *Rebels and Rage: Reflecting on #FeesMustFall*, 'we are the agents of our own liberation' (Habib 2019: 115).

References

Allen, Danielle S. 2004. *Talking to Strangers: Anxieties of Citizenship since Brown v. Board of Education*. Chicago, Illinois: University of Chicago Press.
Habib, Adam. 2019. *Rebels and Rage: Reflecting on #FeesMustFall*. Johannesburg: Jonathan Ball.
Ricœur, Paul. 1965. *History and Truth: Translated with an Introduction by Charles A. Kelbley*. Translated by Charles A. Kelbey. 2nd ed. Evanston, IL: Northwestern University Press.
Ricœur, Paul. 1968. Preface. In *Conceptions de l'université. Jacques Dreze and Jean Debelle*, 8–22. Paris: Éditions Universitaires.
Ricœur, Paul. 2007. *Reflections on the Just*. Translated by David Pellauer. Chicago, Illinois; London: University of Chicago Press.
Taylor, Harry. 2023. Gillian Keegan at Odds with Home Office Plan to Restrict Overseas Students. *The Guardian*, February 11, 2023, sec. Education. https://www.theguardian.com/education/2023/feb/11/overseas-students-restriction-home-office-plan-gillian-keegan.
Ward-Glenton, Hannah. 2022. Foreign Students to Reportedly Be Barred from UK Unless Studying at Top Universities. *CNBC*, November 25, 2022, sec. Europe Politics. https://www.cnbc.com/2022/11/25/foreign-students-to-reportedly-be-barred-from-uk-unless-studying-at-top-universities.html.

Open Access This chapter is licensed under the terms of the Creative Commons Attribution 4.0 International License (http://creativecommons.org/licenses/by/4.0/), which permits use, sharing, adaptation, distribution and reproduction in any medium or format, as long as you give appropriate credit to the original author(s) and the source, provide a link to the Creative Commons license and indicate if changes were made.

The images or other third party material in this chapter are included in the chapter's Creative Commons license, unless indicated otherwise in a credit line to the material. If material is not included in the chapter's Creative Commons license and your intended use is not permitted by statutory regulation or exceeds the permitted use, you will need to obtain permission directly from the copyright holder.

Index

A
Activism, 49, 60, 99–101
Activism/ activist, 3, 4, 10, 11
Addams, J., 7, 8, 10, 11, 36, 37, 41, 102, 103, 105, 108, 114
Adorno, T., 84
Ahsan, S., 24
Aitlhadj, L., 19
Akala, 23
Aked, H., 19
Al-Fihri, F., 27
Algeria, 3, 11
Algeria/ns, 49–52, 54–58, 66, 69
Al Ghazali, Z., 74
Ali, K., 74
Allen, D., 7, 8, 10, 38, 42, 45, 46, 88, 114, 115
All-Party Parliamentary Group (APPG), 100, 109, 110, 115
Al-Qarawiyyin, 27
America/n, 2, 3, 5, 11
American Nazi Party, 82
Andrews, K., 90
Anjum, O., 43, 52, 53
Anti-blackness, 20
Anti-racism, 24
Anti-woke/ woke, 22–24, 94, 114, 116
Aristotle, 114

B
Badenoch, K., 90
Bad infinity, 79, 81, 85, 86, 88, 89, 91
Badiou, A., 84
Begg, M., 74
Bhambra, G. K., 52

Bias blind spot, 81
Binary/ies, 1–4, 8, 9, 12, 50, 57, 59, 60, 99
Black Lives Matter, 22, 24
Black Power protest, 88
Bollo Brook Youth Centre, 109
Briefings (ICOP), 110
British Empire, 23
Butler, J., 39, 40

C
Callicle, 43, 45
Cancel culture, 101
Chakrabarti, S., 110
Charity Commission, 20
Chicago, 1, 3, 7, 8, 11, 79–82, 87–89
Chilling effect, 24
Class, 5, 6, 11, 12
Cohn-Bendit, D., 68, 69
Cole, T., 85, 91, 92
Collini, S., 18
Colonial/ism/ist, 3, 11, 49–56, 60, 62
Commission on Race and Ethnic Disparities, 20
Communities of Inquiry, 4, 5, 8, 10, 11, 33, 36, 37, 39–41, 45, 46, 99–101, 105, 109
Conservative, 2, 9
Coulthard, G., 91
Covid-19, 101, 108
Critical Race Theory (CRT), 23, 90
Cultural imaginations, 101
Culture of poverty, 87
Culture wars, 2–4, 7, 21–24, 33, 38, 39, 114–116
Curriculum, 23, 25, 27

D

Danisch, R., 103–105
Dars-i Niẓāmī, 27, 28
Dean, 65, 68, 69
Decolonisation, 24, 55, 61, 62
Decolonising, 114
De Gaulle, C., 67, 73
Democratic rights, 110
Derrida, J., 83
Desert/ion, 56, 60
De Tocqueville, A., 52
Dewey, J., 36
Dialectic/al, 3, 4, 8–10, 53, 57, 84, 85, 99, 100
Discrimination, 79–82, 87, 90–92
Dogra, S., 81
Donelan, M., 93, 94
Dosse, F., 17
Doyle, A., 22
Dubitative form, 37
Duffy, B., 21, 24
Durkheim, E., 52

E

Ebony initiative, 109
Eckford, E., 105
Eddo-Lodge, R., 22
El Fadl, K. A., 74
Elshayyal, K., 20, 21
Empire, 2, 5, 6
Equality Act, 34
Equality Act 2010, 24
Equality, Diversity and Inclusion (EDI), 15, 24
Esposti, E., 27
Ethics, 33, 37, 38
Existentialism/t, 50, 53, 54, 60

F

Faloyin, D., 61
Fanon, F., 55, 89, 90
Faust, J. R., 89
Fiṭra, 43
Floyd, George, 24
Foucault, M., 73
Fowler, C., 23
Freedom of expression, 110
Free speech, 2, 5, 6, 9, 10, 33, 34, 37, 40, 80, 83, 90, 93, 94, 114–116
French
　army, 56
　public opinion, 55
　state, 56, 57
　union, 55
Freud, S., 69–72
Funding, 16, 28

G

Geertz, C., 57
Gender, 65, 70, 73, 74
Gender identity, 5
General Social Survey (GSS), 80
Gentleman, A., 80
Global majority, 3
Gorgias, 42, 43, 46
Graeco-Arabic translation movement, 44
Grappin, P., 68
Great replacement theory, 21, 22
Greek dialectics, 27
Group
　cohesion, 42
　decision-making, 36, 42
　influence, 42
Guarded liberal, 5, 39

H

Habermas, J., 27, 28, 33–35, 37, 38
Hallaq, W., 23, 25, 50–53, 58
Hall, S., 8
Health, 80, 81
Hegel, G., 70, 84, 86, 102
Hegel, W., 3
Heinze, E., 23
Hermeneutics of suspicion, 66, 70–72, 75
HE sector, 9, 115
Higher Education (Freedom of Speech) Act, 9, 23
Higher Education Policy Institute (HEPI), 34
Hillman, N., 34
Hiwār, 42
Hobbes, J., 102
Holmwood, J., 19, 52
Honneth, A., 89
Horkheimer, M., 3
Hull House, 105
Human rights, 5
Hume, D., 102
Hunter, J. D., 21

I

Identity, 79–81, 83, 85–87, 89–91
Identity crises, 71

Index 121

Identity politics, 2–4
Ideology, 53, 57, 58
Ideology of difference, 87, 89
Imputability, 104
In/justice, 52–54
Inequality/ies, 5, 6
Influencing the Corridors of Power (ICOP), 100, 108–110, 115, 116
Insubordination, 55, 56, 60
Iranian revolution, 26
Islam/ic, 74, 106, 107
Islamicate, 27
Islamophobia, 5

J
James, W., 36
Jaspers, K., 15
Jim Crow, 82
Jones, S., 17, 28
Justice, 102

K
Kalām, 27
Kant, I., 33–35, 38, 82, 83, 92
Kaufmann, E., 21

L
Laïcité/ secularism, 26
Lawrence, S., 22
Legislation, 9, 10
Lewis, O., 87
Liberal, 2, 5, 15, 17, 18, 23, 27, 28, 38, 39
Liberation, 117
Libertarian/ism, 2, 3, 5, 7, 9, 37–39
Linguistic, 53, 58, 59
Lipsitz, G., 2
Logical contradiction, 83, 84
Louvain, University of, 79
Lu-Adler, H., 35

M
Malik, K., 4
Marxism/t, 18
Marx, K., 52, 57, 70–72
Matryoshka dolls, 4, 100
Media, 21, 22
Modernity, 25
Mohdin, Walker and Parveen, 20
Moosa, E., 50, 51
Morsi, Y., 23

Mu'tazilites, 27
Mudde C and Kaltwasser C, 1
Munāzara, 43
Murad, A., 15, 25
Muslim, 7, 12, 49, 50, 53, 56, 57

N
Naguib, S., 26, 74
Nanterre, 3, 17–19, 65, 66, 68–71, 73, 75, 79, 87
Nation-state, 52, 54
Negation/ negative, 57, 58, 60, 80, 81, 83, 84, 86
Newman, Cardinal John Henry, 18
Nietzsche, F., 70–72
1968, 2, 5, 6, 10, 11, 15, 17, 19, 65–71, 73, 75
No-platforming, 5, 9, 21, 25, 39, 101

O
O'Connor, P., 38
Office for Students, 101
Olusoga, D., 23
Optative form, 37
Oratory, 43, 44
Orwell, G., 92

P
Palfreyman, D and Temple, P., 16
Parliament, 4
Parliamentarians, 100–102, 109
Partnerships, 107
Pedagogy, 26
Peirce, C. S., 36
Perfect, S., 20
Phenomenological distress, 72
Phenomenology/ical, 50, 53, 54, 58–60, 70
Piketty, T., 6
Pincer grip/s, 3, 4, 9
Pincourt, C and Lindsay, J., 22
Police, 66, 68, 69
Political friendship, 7, 104, 105
Politics of pedagogy, 4, 10, 11, 99–101, 105–108
Politics of recognition, 86, 88, 91
Polity praxis, 4, 11, 27, 99, 100, 105, 107, 109
Populism, populist, 1, 2, 6–9, 12, 72, 73, 83, 84
Populism's Pincer Grip, 39
Poverty, 80–82, 87

Pragmatism/t, 4, 5, 7, 8, 10, 11
Pragmatist philosophy, 37
Prevent, 15, 19, 20, 22
Procedural ethics, 38–40
Protest, 101, 102, 108, 110
Protestant, 52
Public Order Bill, 100, 102, 110

Q
Qur'an, 44

R
Racism, racist, race, 2, 3, 5–7, 9–12, 35, 40, 80–82, 86, 87, 89–93
Ramsey, F., 103, 104
Rawls, J., 82
Religion, 7, 8, 81, 99, 106
Rhetoric, 4, 7, 8, 10–12, 42–46
Rhetorical pragmatism, 103, 104
Right wing, 9

S
Sacrifice, 105
Sallenave, D., 23
Sartre, J-P., 53, 55, 56, 60
Savage, M., 6
Science, Technology, Engineering and Maths (STEM), 16, 28
Scharbrodt, O., 26, 51
Scott-Baumann, A., 16, 20, 22, 26, 27
Secular, 106
Secularism, 26
Self-censorship, 16
Sexually neutral thesis, 73
Sexual revolution, 70
Shari'a, 50, 51
Shi'ism, 26, 27
Slavery, 2, 3, 23
Social media, 6
Socrates, 42–45
Sorbonne, 3, 11, 65–69, 72, 79
Sovereignty, 84
Standpoint epistemology, 102
State, 17, 19, 20, 23, 25, 26, 28
Stepek, J., 5
Structuralism/ists, 50, 53, 54, 56, 59
Structural racism, 6
Sunni, 26, 27

T
Táíwò, O., 62
Taşköprüzāde, A. K., 27, 28, 44
Taylor, C., 87, 90–92
Theology of domination, 53
Theory of recognition, 89
Titley, G., 23
Tricontinental conference, 69
Trigger warning, 86, 94

U
Unhappy consciousness, 85, 86, 92
Universalism/t, 4, 7
Universities UK UUK, 93
USA, 17, 21, 22, 114
Utopia, 57, 58, 110

V
Vietnam, 5, 66, 69
Vinding, N.V., 51

W
War, 49, 51, 52, 54–56, 61
Weber, M., 52, 102
Wesseley, S., 80
Westminster, 108–110, 115, 116
Whitehead, S., 38
Whiteness, 81, 90, 99
White privilege, 2
Wilkerson, I., 22
Wilson, A., 22
Windrush, 80

The manufacturer's authorised representative in the EU is Springer Nature Customer Service Centre GmbH, Europaplatz 3, 69115 Heidelberg, Germany. If you have any concerns regarding our products, please contact ProductSafety@springernature.com

Printed and bound by CPI Group (UK) Ltd, Croydon, CR0 4YY

23/03/2026

02076360-0016